# GUID...

C000097888

Edited by **David Spriggs**

**The Bible Reading Fellowship**
15 The Chambers, Vineyard
Abingdon OX14 3FE
brf.org.uk

The Bible Reading Fellowship (BRF) is a Registered Charity (233280)

ISBN 978 0 85746 649 5
All rights reserved

This edition © The Bible Reading Fellowship 2018
Cover image © Thinkstock

Distributed in Australia by:
MediaCom Education Inc, PO Box 610, Unley, SA 5061
Tel: 1 800 811 311 | admin@mediacom.org.au

Distributed in New Zealand by:
Scripture Union Wholesale, PO Box 760, Wellington
Tel: 04 385 0421 | suwholesale@clear.net.nz

**Acknowledgements**
Scripture quotations taken from The Holy Bible, New International Version (Anglicised edition) copyright © 1979, 1984, 2011 by Biblica. Used by permission of Hodder & Stoughton Publishers, a Hachette UK company. All rights reserved. 'NIV' is a registered trademark of Biblica. UK trademark number 1448790. • Scripture quotations taken from the Holy Bible, English Standard Version, published by HarperCollins Publishers, © 2001 Crossway Bibles, a division of Good News Publishers. Used by permission. All rights reserved. • Scripture quotations from The New Revised Standard Version of the Bible, Anglicised edition, copyright © 1989, 1995 by the Division of Christian Education of the National Council of the Churches of Christ in the United States of America. Used by permission. All rights reserved. • Extracts from the Authorised Version of the Bible (The King James Bible), the rights in which are vested in the Crown, are reproduced by permission of the Crown's Patentee, Cambridge University Press. • Scripture quotations taken from the New American Standard Bible®, Copyright © 1960, 1962, 1963, 1968, 1971, 1972, 1973, 1975, 1977, 1995 by The Lockman Foundation. Used by permission. (www.Lockman.org) • Scripture quotations are taken from The Message, copyright © 1993, 1994, 1995, 1996, 2000, 2001, 2002 by Eugene H. Peterson. Used by permission of NavPress. All rights reserved. Represented by Tyndale House Publishers, Inc. • Scripture quotations taken from the Amplified® Bible (AMP), Copyright © 2015 by The Lockman Foundation. Used by permission. www.Lockman.org • Scripture quotations from the New Life Version of the Bible copyright © 1969 by Christian Literature International.

Every effort has been made to trace and contact copyright owners for material used in this resource. We apologise for any inadvertent omissions or errors, and would ask those concerned to contact us so that full acknowledgement can be made in the future.

Printed by Gutenberg Press, Tarxien, Malta

# Suggestions for using *Guidelines*

Set aside a regular time and place, if possible, when and where you can read and pray undisturbed. Before you begin, take time to be still and, if you find it helpful, use the BRF Prayer on page 6.

In *Guidelines*, the introductory section provides context for the passages or themes to be studied, while the units of comment can be used daily, weekly, or whatever best fits your timetable. You will need a Bible (more than one if you want to compare different translations) as Bible passages are not included. At the end of each week is a 'Guidelines' section, offering further thoughts about or practical application of what you have been studying.

Occasionally, you may read something in *Guidelines* that you find particularly challenging, even uncomfortable. This is inevitable in a series of notes which draws on a wide spectrum of contributors, and doesn't believe in ducking difficult issues. Indeed, we believe that *Guidelines* readers much prefer thought-provoking material to a bland diet that only confirms what they already think.

If you do disagree with a contributor, you may find it helpful to go through these three steps. First, think about why you feel uncomfortable. Perhaps this is an idea that is new to you, or you are not happy about the way something has been expressed. Or there may be something more substantial – you may feel that the writer is guilty of sweeping generalisation, factual error, or theological or ethical misjudgement. Second, pray that God would use this disagreement to teach you more about his word and about yourself. Third, think about what you will do as a result of the disagreement. You might resolve to find out more about the issue, or write to the contributor or the editor of *Guidelines*.

To send feedback, please email **enquiries@brf.org.uk**, phone **+44 (0)1865 319700** or write to the address shown opposite.

# Writers in this issue

From 2014 to 2017, **Martin Lee** was Director of Global Connections, a UK network of churches and agencies that long to see mission placed at the heart of the church. He now works as a consultant with a variety of charities.

**Steve Walton** is a researcher and teacher of the New Testament. He is an Anglican priest, and has served in student ministry and parish ministry. Steve has published a number of books and articles.

**Pauline Hoggarth** was born in Peru. She has served with Scripture Union in three different roles in the UK and overseas. She is the author of *The Seed and the Soil: Engaging with the word of God* (Langham, 2011).

**Brian Howell** is visiting lecturer in Old Testament at London School of Theology. Previously he served as the Dean of Studies for Bible Society. He has published on interpreting divine metaphors, and currently researches the *Imago Dei* when not playing saxophone.

**John Rackley** is a Baptist minister. He has held positions with the BBC, Baptist Union, Retreat Association and Churches Together in England. As a Spiritual Director, he leads retreats and blogs at **windingquest.wordpress.com**.

**Torsten Uhlig** is currently a teacher of the Old Testament. Previously, he served as a pastor in the Lutheran Church of Saxony, Germany for eight years. He loves both ministries.

**Andrew Mayes** is Spirituality Adviser to the Diocese of Cyprus and the Gulf and parish priest of Limassol. An associate professor of St George's College Jerusalem, he has lived in the Holy Land and is the author of several books.

**Jill Duff** is Bishop of Lancaster, with responsibility for mission, evangelism and church planting in the diocese of Blackburn. Previously, she was Director of St Mellitus NW (where she taught New Testament and Mission) and has planted several congregations in diverse contexts.

**David Spriggs** provides occasional consultancy services for Bible Society, but his main role is as a Baptist minister again. He is a part-time minister with the Friar Lane and Braunstone Baptist Church, Leicester.

**Ian Paul** is Associate Minister at St Nic's Nottingham, and Honorary Assistant Professor at the University of Nottingham, as well as Managing Editor at Grove Books in Cambridge. He blogs at **psephizo.com**.

# David Spriggs writes...

I wonder which of the gospels is your favourite. I am especially attracted to Luke so I'm looking forward to this year's lectionary gospel notes. We are guided through the second half of this gospel by Dr Steve Walton and so will have the opportunity to see it with fresh eyes and discover new and significant things about Jesus the Saviour as we follow his journey to the cross. Inevitably, we will gain fresh insights about our own leadership and mission.

We begin this issue with 'Leadership for kingdom building', written by Martin Lee. He will utilise his knowledge of the church worldwide as well as his own experience of leading Christian organisations to share with us the challenges, pitfalls and opportunities of those who are called to be leaders in the Christian community.

Pauline Hoggarth is a new writer. She takes us on the journey with Naomi and Ruth. At one level, this is a delightful 'country story', but it is also strangely relevant today; the plotline is about migration, death, poverty and vulnerability. Within and beyond this, there is the action of God, who rescues even in these terrifying circumstances.

Brian Howell engages us with the stories of the patriarchs as they unfold in Genesis 12—36. In his reflections, he brings us further personal challenges.

We have a specific Lent focus from John Rackley, a Baptist minister, who has led many conferences. This is his first contribution. He takes us on a spiritual pilgrimage as he explores various 'pathways'.

Then, let me introduce you to Torsten Uhlig, another new author, who lectures in Germany. He focuses on some core themes in Isaiah.

In addition to this wealth of contributions, Dr Andrew Mayes (Third Order, Society of St Francis) encourages us to use the Bible to deepen our spirituality. He opens our eyes (perhaps it would be more appropriate to say, 'our five senses') to the intense physicality of the fourth gospel as a means of appreciating the reality of the incarnation. At the same time, he brings deep challenges to us to develop our own spirituality.

As we approach the end of Lent, Jill Duff's helpful reflections on women, especially those we meet in Luke's gospel, will complement this focus. To help us travel through Holy Week, I have looked at the leadership pressures Jesus was under as he moved towards the cross.

Then Ian Paul takes on the baton as he looks backwards from the perspective of Acts at the resurrection. This serves to remind us that all the New Testament is a 'post-Easter' document and that the resurrection is at the centre of our redemption and has impact and implications for the Christian church throughout all time.

# The BRF Prayer

*Almighty God,*
*you have taught us that your word is a lamp for our feet*
*and a light for our path. Help us, and all who prayerfully*
*read your word, to deepen our fellowship with you*
*and with each other through your love.*
*And in so doing may we come to know you more fully,*
*love you more truly, and follow more faithfully*
*in the steps of your son Jesus Christ, who lives and reigns*
*with you and the Holy Spirit, one God for evermore.*
*Amen*

# Leadership for kingdom building

Martin Lee

Who springs to mind when you are asked, 'Who is the greatest leader you have come across?' What criteria do you use? How successful they were or, more subjectively, how they treated you? Or do we measure them by their charismatic personality?

How do we judge what success looks like for a Christian leader? Is it someone whose ministry has grown exponentially? Is it only larger and growing churches or ministries that are successful?

So much is written about leadership. There are hundreds of books, thousands of articles and countless consultants, all seeking to help leaders lead well. Yet so much of what is taught to those involved in Christian leadership is based on business and secular principles. Lots of it is really good stuff and extremely helpful and we cannot ignore the best of what society at large can teach us. I have benefited enormously from understanding change theory and my role in change. I have had great fun understanding more about myself and working out if I was an owl, a fox, a teddy bear or a shark!

However, in the scriptures and especially in the life of Jesus, we have a depth of material to learn from. My leadership was revolutionised by some talks I heard from Ajith Fernando, the Director of Youth for Christ in Sri Lanka. The western world may have produced its books and thinks it has all the answers, but we often fail to listen to leaders from non-western settings. Our western culture focuses on comfort, self-satisfaction, good feelings and 'success'. However, the world of the New Testament was so different to ours; Ajith's thesis is that even a quick glance at the New Testament shows that the cross of suffering is an essential part of Christian ministry. Somehow, we seem to have lost that in our individualistic and self-centred society.

Christian leadership has at its heart the marks of suffering. This is not because of stress due to overwork or crazy schedules. Rather, it is about the need to deny ourselves and follow him (Mark 8:34), yearning for those in our care (Galatians 4:19), honouring others more than ourselves (Romans 12:10) and wanting God's glory alone (John 3:30).

Unless otherwise stated, quotations are from the New International Version (Anglicised).

# 1 Character is key

**Philippians 2:1–8**

There are thousands of opinions about what make a good leader. One idea is that leaders need to show the four Cs – competence, calling, confidence and character. There is no question that leaders need to be very competent, have a clear vision and have a confident 'can-do' attitude. Incompetent leaders who do not know where they are going and are risk-averse will end up leading nowhere.

Whatever we do and however we lead, God is ultimately more interested in our character than anything else. Smart business techniques, clear strategy and drive might be important, but God is much more concerned about integrity and faithfulness. 'The righteous lead blameless lives; blessed are their children after them' (Proverbs 20:7). 'At this, the chief ministers and the satraps tried to find grounds for charges against Daniel in his conduct of government affairs, but they were unable to do so. They could find no corruption in him, because he was trustworthy and neither corrupt nor negligent' (Daniel 6:4).

A Christian leader needs to be the same in public as in private. At home, at work, when relaxing or in church, it doesn't matter. There will be consistency and a deep longing to be more and more like Jesus. Position will mean nothing and promotion won't change them. A successful business or church will not go to their heads.

Philippians 2 takes us to the real marks of the character needed in Christian leadership, as it looks to Christ's example. A Christian leader will do nothing from selfish ambition, is not conceited, values his (or her – I use male pronouns throughout for ease) colleagues and congregation highly, and looks to the interests of others.

If a Christian leader focuses solely on his own natural innate ability as a leader and forgets the command to live a godly life, he disqualifies himself as a leader. 'Now the overseer is to be above reproach, faithful to his wife, temperate, self-controlled, respectable, hospitable, able to teach, not given to drunkenness, not violent but gentle, not quarrelsome, not a lover of money' (1 Timothy 3:2–3).

How we live as leaders is key and, at the end of the day, we should focus on having the mindset of Christ Jesus. It is about denying ourselves the acclaim of position and not using position to one's own advantage. It is about living a life that becomes 'obedient to death' (v. 8). I wonder how that expresses itself for me as a leader?

# 2 Influence

John 13:1–17

Any leader will want to get the best out of their team of followers. Excellent orientation, for both newcomers and old-stagers, is essential, as there is always room for development. However, there is one simple key truth: people learn by example, not by telling. Instead of telling people what to do, show them by your own example. Practise deeply what you preach, and the results will astonish you. Especially during difficult times, when everyone wants to give up, you should be the one who faces obstacles with confidence and determination towards success. You will find even those whom you thought were the weakest will do the same and stand by your side.

The well-known story in John about Jesus washing his disciples' feet exemplifies this. Before a meal, foot-washing was common due to the dusty and dirty conditions and the wearing of sandals. Such foot-washing was undertaken by the lowliest of menial servants and peers did not wash one another's feet. Maybe the disciples might have been happy to wash Jesus' feet, but they would not even conceive of washing each other's feet. When Jesus moved to wash their feet, they were astonished. By doing this, Jesus taught the lesson of selfless service that should be the mark of Christian leadership.

Sadly, in wider society, many seem to think that influence comes by being overpowering, belittling, manipulating, threatening, competing or controlling. Few follow the Jesus way. Leading by example like this can influence others to behave in a Christlike manner. Paul urges the younger men in Titus 2:7–8 (ESV) to 'show yourself in all respects to be a model of good works, and in your teaching show integrity, dignity, and sound speech that cannot be condemned, so that an opponent may be put to shame, having nothing evil to say about us.' Leaders need to lead through serving by modelling, encouraging, training and especially releasing. Allow those whom you are leading to make mistakes, and be ready to come alongside them and wash their feet if it all goes wrong.

Leadership is not only about getting something done; leadership is seeing people change, being empowered and growing. Ultimately, leadership is seeing people developed. Godly influence and example are the best way, far better than any amount of skill, business technique or control. A leader's prime role is guiding followers to become more and more like Christ. 'Be imitators of me, as I am of Christ' (1 Corinthians 11:1, ESV).

# 3 Commitment to developing others

**Matthew 20:20–28**

In British culture, we are not good at praising success and we certainly don't like it when people 'get ahead of themselves'. Here in our story, the mother of James and John asks for 'promotion' for them to key leadership positions. Jesus' reaction is so illuminating. Rather than taking them to task, Jesus says it will require enormous sacrifice on their part, which, from their reaction, they obviously don't comprehend. When the other disciples hear about it, any sense of team has been destroyed and James and John feel the wrath of the group.

Jesus uses the opportunity to teach about real leadership. He doesn't fume or get exasperated by the request or the team's reaction; instead, he turns leadership upside down. Look at verses 27–28: 'Whoever wants to be first must be your slave – just as the Son of Man did not come to be served, but to serve, and to give his life as a ransom for many.'

We hear a lot about 'servant leadership' but Jesus calls us to 'laying down our lives' leadership. 'Greater love has no one than this: to lay down one's life for one's friends' (John 15:13). Christian leaders are those who will treat their congregation or their staff as friends and are prepared to go to any length to nurture, support and serve them.

Leaders can often have difficult followers and it is when people don't live up to our hopes and expectations that true leaders come into their own. When we are committed to those whom we lead (or rather serve), we don't bad-mouth them, demote them, shout at them or allow our frustration to cloud our judgement.

'I am the good shepherd. The good shepherd lays down his life for the sheep. The hired hand is not the shepherd and does not own the sheep. So when he sees the wolf coming, he abandons the sheep and runs away' (John 10:11–12). True Christian leadership does not run away from the flock when the going gets tough.

Leading is getting a vision accomplished, but true leadership is about far more than this. To get a vision accomplished but burn out our followers is to fail as a leader. True success is really in the building up of others. To do that, we need to be a critical friend, understanding their temperaments, respecting their concerns, believing in their gifts and supporting their dreams. At the same time, we also need to be able to challenge flaws by honesty, encouragement and coming alongside.

# 4 Prayer

**John 17:6–19**

It is so easy to get burnt out in Christian service. There are some fantastic resources around on dealing with stress and I have benefited from many of them enormously. Expectations can be high and we can put undue pressure on ourselves, working long hours for success. Stress can also come as result of intense competition. Leaders are driven people and, in our unbiblical society, we can adopt a 'messiah complex'. We end up bearing burdens that are not ours. That is not the sort of burden or stress that leaders should experience.

Stress can often be the result of a lack of rest and prayer. Mark 1:35 says: 'Very early in the morning… Jesus got up, left the house and went off to a solitary place, where he prayed.' Christ would often get away from the crowd to pray. He knew the importance of spending time with God alone. Reflect for a while on Matthew 14:23 or Luke 6:12. Leaders need to build in time for retreat, reflection and refreshment.

Yet pressure and stress is part and parcel of the leadership package. 2 Corinthians 11:28 tells us Paul's situation: 'Besides everything else, I face daily the pressure of my concern for all the churches.' Pressure and stress will come inevitably, but this should be out of a love for others and not a lust for achievement. It is the result of identifying closely with people and being concerned for their welfare.

Christ knew the importance of praying for those in his care. Verses 11–12 in our reading are all about praying for protection for his followers, as is verse 15. Even when we are stressed, our focus for prayer needs to be about those whom God has given us to lead. The whole of the reading exemplifies his concern for his followers. In Colossians 4:13, Paul commends Epaphras for 'always wrestling in prayer for you, that you may stand firm in all the will of God, mature and fully assured'.

We may have the stress of love, but we can't have the anxiety of unbelief. 'Do not be anxious about anything, but in every situation, by prayer and petition, with thanksgiving, present your requests to God. And the peace of God, which transcends all understanding, will guard your hearts and your minds in Christ Jesus' (Philippians 4:6–7). We grapple with God in prayer until we have cast our burden on him. We are released from its power over us, and our joy and rest are restored.

# 5  Still a learner

1 Corinthians 4:1–7

Verses 1–2 contain an exhortation to be faithful with the trust God has given us. In my previous position, I often spent times in countries like the Philippines. One of my best friends there was a young man called Nathaniel. He looks on me as a mentor, but for me his faithfulness, prayer life and dependence on God are just some things that I aspire to have just a little more of. At one time, some of his family turned on him and tried to oust him from his leadership role in a children's ministry. His quiet acceptance of what happened, warmth to those who wronged him and prayer for the best to come out of the situation have remained with me since. Eventually, after nearly two years, he was restored and the ministry has flourished. He was completely faithful, yet did not usurp anyone. I am sure that we all know people like that – rather than me being his mentor, he has been my mentor and inspiration.

A true leader will have no desire to lord it over others, but will be faithful, humble, gentle, self-sacrificing and as ready to follow as to lead. He will not usurp any position but will be faithful and true. A true leader wants to learn in all situations and from others.

There is a useful training technique called the Johari Window, which is about learning more about oneself from others and opening up oneself to others. I have realised that we are never too old, our ministry never too large, our experiences never too many and our knowledge never too much for us to be able to learn from people who are younger, less experienced, less educated, from different backgrounds or from different theological positions.

Leadership is an ever-learning experience. 'Instruct the wise and they will be wiser still; teach the righteous and they will add to their learning' (Proverbs 9:9). 'Let the wise listen and add to their learning, and let the discerning get guidance' (Proverbs 1:5).

As our reading reflects in verse 7: 'For who makes you different from anyone else? What do you have that you did not receive? And if you did receive it, why do you boast as though you did not?' A wise leader will not think of himself more highly than he ought, but will seek to learn from others and with others.

# 6 Decrease and increase

John 3:22–30

In her book *These Strange Ashes* (Revell, 2004), Elizabeth Elliot, the widow of Jim Elliot of the Auca tribe fame, reflects on their early years of ministry before they married. The book shares her sense of failure after two years of hard work was seemingly destroyed: her language notes fell off a lorry and Jim's building work was swept away in a flood. At the end, she recounts an African legend about Jesus walking with his disciples. He asked each one to pick up a stone to carry for him. Peter picked up a small one and John a bigger one. Jesus then commanded the stones to be made bread. Of course, Peter didn't have very much while John had more than enough to share. Soon after, Jesus took the same disciples for another walk and again asked them to pick up a stone to carry for him. As you can imagine, Peter picked up a huge boulder this time. Then, after a long walk, he told them to throw the stones down. Nothing happened and they waited and waited. Jesus, with great compassion, looked on these disciples whom he loved and said, 'For whom did you carry the stone?'

It is of course a completely made-up story. However, in our reading, we learn something special about John the Baptist. Already his followers are leaving him to follow this new teacher. Soon, he will be beheaded and his ministry will fade away. Of course, he is very aware of the fact that Jesus is the one for whom he was making the path straight. Yet his simple statement

'He must increase, but I must decrease' (v. 30, ESV) gets to the heart of what ministry should all be about.

For me, this has been the hardest leadership lesson ever. Several years ago, my own agency, which had been a market leader, suddenly lost a substantial part of its support base and key personnel. I had spent a lot of time helping other agencies in the spirit of cooperation and wanting the best for them – all good Christian attitudes. However, those agencies suddenly started to attract the funding that had previously come our way and several people moved to work for the competition at a higher rate of pay. My own agency looked like it might not survive. Was this poor leadership on my part? I remember crying as my world collapsed, and at that low moment God spoke almost audibly: 'You must decrease that I might increase.' It was a hard lesson, but strangely liberating and life-changing. 'Whatever you do, do it all for the glory of God' (1 Corinthians 10:31).

## Guidelines

Consider which of the following presents the greatest challenge for you. Pray about it and ask friends to help you grow into it.

* There is much excellent leadership material around today. However, we need to reflect especially on the scriptural examples of leadership where the basis of leadership is very different to that in wider society. 'Follow God's example, therefore, as dearly loved children and live a life of love, just as Christ loved us and gave himself up for us as a fragrant offering and sacrifice to God' (Ephesians 5:1–2). Our example should be such that we can confidently say, 'Be imitators of me as I am of Christ' (1 Corinthians 11:1, ESV).

* We need to be open-hearted with all and know people well enough so that we can get alongside with love. Yes, it is about sacrifice and laying down our lives, but only by being loving friends. At the great Edinburgh missionary conference in 1910, Revd V.S. Azariah from South India concluded: 'Through all the ages to come, the Indian Church will rise up in gratitude to attest the heroism and self-denying labours of the missionary body. You have given your goods to feed the poor. You have given your bodies to be burned. We also ask for love. Give us FRIENDS!'

- Leaders need to keep themselves fresh and full of the joy of the Lord. Leadership is full of pressure, but that pressure needs to be that of feeling responsibility for others' welfare. If dependence on prayer was important to Jesus, how much more to us? We need to be constantly learning from others, never ever thinking that we have arrived because we have achieved this or that. We need to sit at the feet of children and learn from them.

Perhaps, though, our greatest challenge is to consider what motivates us to lead. Ministry is not about success, nor is it about building the largest church or the best agency, attracting the most donations or preaching the greatest sermon. It is about seeing God alone glorified, even if our part is never seen or acknowledged, or even if what we have done seems to have been destroyed.

# Luke 14—18

## Steve Walton

This section of Luke sees Jesus on the road to Jerusalem, a way he's been heading since he 'set his face' to go there (9:51). We encounter him travelling south from his home territory of Galilee, along the border between Samaria and Galilee (17:11), and then crossing the river Jordan by Jericho (18:35) to press on to the big city, where his destiny will be fulfilled (18:31–34). Three threads keep recurring in this journey, and they are things to look out for as the section develops.

First, Luke includes in this section much that is unique to his telling of the biography of Jesus, especially many well-known parables: the lost coin, the two lost sons, the crooked manager, the rich man and Lazarus, and the Pharisee and the tax collector. In these stories, Luke invites us to enter the right-side-up world of the kingdom of God, whose values and attitudes are the reverse of the world's way.

Second, we also hear some remarkable stories of Jesus, again frequently uniquely Lukan, which highlight key features of Jesus' mission and ministry: his table manners and the company he keeps are shocking to the established Jewish leaders, because he hangs out with and welcomes 'sinners'; he explicitly and implicitly criticises those who attack him as in serious error; he welcomes even tiny babies; he claims that the whole story of scripture points forward to him and his proclamation of God's reign. The Jesus of these chapters puts himself at the centre of God's purposes.

Third, Jesus offers great challenge in this section – then and now – as his call to discipleship is stated and restated, unpacked and expanded. The challenge of following Jesus is clear here: it costs no less than everything, and in particular demands a transformed attitude to money and possessions – they are to be placed at the Master's disposal.

Unless otherwise stated, quotations are from the New Revised Standard Version.

14 January–3 February

# 1 To heal or not to heal – on the sabbath?

**Luke 14:1–6**

Going to eat in a different social setting can be very difficult. Are you using the right knife and fork? Are you being rude by taking food before someone else? Table manners are a big issue in cultures where meals are about social bonding, as in first-century Palestine. The people you ate with, and those who ate with you, were key markers of your social standing.

This is the third time Jesus eats with Pharisees in Luke (see 7:36–50; 11:37–54), and here it is with a Pharisaic leader (v. 1). The meal is on a sabbath, probably a midday meal following the synagogue meeting. Luke's observation that Jesus was being watched sets the scene: will Jesus act and speak in ways which show he is 'in' or 'out' with the Pharisees?

The man with dropsy may have been brought in by the host as a test for Jesus – or he may just have wandered in because Jesus was around: meals were semi-public events in that culture and people frequently stood around the edges of the room to listen in. Dropsy ('an abnormal swelling of his body', NIV) involves part of the body swelling because of fluid retention; it is not usually life-threatening (unless a sign of heart or kidney failure), but it is unpleasant and socially awkward. Certainly, the Pharisees knew Jesus' reputation for associating with those whom they regarded as social outcasts: what would he do?

Jesus' question (v. 3) highlights a debate concerning the commandment which forbade work on the sabbath (Exodus 20:10). But what counted as 'work'? We know the Qumran sect (who wrote the Dead Sea Scrolls) forbade helping an animal out of a pit on the sabbath (compare v. 5), and yet some of the later rabbis allowed it. Jesus' question opposed rigid interpretations of the sabbath law – surely the sabbath, the day set aside for the worship of God and for rest, was the most appropriate day on which to heal!

Jesus then exposed the Pharisees' hypocrisy by observing that they would surely help a child or an ox out of a well on the sabbath. The people who set out to 'watch' Jesus (v. 1) found the tables turned on them – he questioned their thinking and pointed them to the generous grace of God to people in need.

# 2 Upside-down values at a banquet

Luke 14:7-14

Here is a classic example of the proverb 'pride goes before a fall'. First-century Palestinian culture was focused around values of honour and shame, and everyone strove to be honoured. To gain honour, you could advertise your achievements and the good things you had done in a way that many today would consider to be 'showing off' – but that was accepted and even encouraged then. Thus, the nearer you sat to the host of a banquet, the more honourable your position was considered to be – and if you arrived early for the banquet, you would naturally head for the highest place available (v. 7), and then watch as others envied you!

For Jesus, the whole premise of the honour and shame culture is rejected, for greatness comes through humility. People who take a high place for themselves are thinking entirely the wrong way – and will get their comeuppance when they have overstepped the mark and are told they must move to a lower seat (vv. 8–9). Jesus' advice might seem to be trying to prevent people making social blunders, but there's more to it than that – for in the real world it is assertive and pushy people who get their own way. But the kingdom of God is not like that – only in Jesus' kingdom will 'the meek… inherit the earth' (Matthew 5:5). So Jesus' promise that humble people will be exalted (v. 11) is true in God's economy, not in the merely human sphere.

We've heard this set of upside-down values before in Luke, in the Magnificat, where the powerful are brought down and the lowly lifted up (1:52), and we shall hear it again (e.g. the rich man and Lazarus, 16:19–31). Rather than being tempted to see as the world sees, and to treat as friends those who are well-known or rich or powerful, Jesus invites his host to be open-handed and generous in his invitations (vv. 12–13) because in the world to come God will reward those who welcome people who are poor, disabled, blind or lame.

# 3 'I cannot come!'

Luke 14:15–24

Here is a third story set at the same dinner party hosted by the Pharisees' leader (14:1), as one guest shows considerable understanding (v. 15). This person picks up the biblical image of the world to come as a joyful 'messianic banquet' (e.g. Isaiah 25:6–8) and associates it with Jesus' teaching about the kingdom of God – God's reign which is beginning to be seen through Jesus and which will be fully seen in the age to come.

Jesus affirms the banquet image and confirms that the kingdom of God is like a banquet. In fact, it's just like a formal banquet of the period, where invitations were sent out and accepted a considerable time in advance, so that the host knew how much food and drink to provide – but the guests did not come to the banquet until the host's servants came to tell them everything was ready (for an example, see Esther 5:8; 6:14). At that point, it was very embarrassing for the host if the guests declined to come, for their earlier acceptance was a solemn commitment to be there.

Thus the guests who declined to come when the host's slave came calling for them (v. 17) portray people who initially respond positively to the kingdom invitation of Jesus, but who later turn back (vv. 18–20). The excuses given are, of course, unreasonable – typically of parables, this one involves unlikely events.

Those whom the host then calls are the same people mentioned earlier (14:13) as those who should be invited to a kingdom-shaped banquet: people in poverty and people with disabilities, including blindness or lameness. The Qumran community thought such people would be excluded from the messianic banquet, but Jesus welcomes them. Jesus goes further, and wants anyone to come who is available – the slave is even to force them to come (v. 23)!

The reality is that people have the chance to respond to the kingdom invitation, and yet it is the surprising people who do this. Those who might have been expected to be there will be excluded. Yes, the kingdom of God is about God's generous welcome, even extending to those in the streets and alleys (v. 23), but also 'the kingdom of God is for the committed, not the dilettante' (R.T. France). The book of Acts will go on to show that it is Gentiles who are the surprising accepters of the invitation, not the Jewish people who might have been expected to accept.

# 4 Family values – or not!

Jesus continues here to underline the point he has just made about the need for persistence in commitment to the kingdom (14:16–24). Failure in discipleship has tragic consequences, and so Jesus warns against them.

The images he uses are striking and go against established cultural values. Your family was your 'nearest and dearest' (as we say), and commitment to them was unquestioned in that day – and in ours in much of the world. Jesus states the point baldly: his disciples must 'hate' their family (v. 26). He uses exaggeration to make a point, as in the preceding parable, and uses 'hate' to mean 'love less' (see 16:13 and compare Malachi 1:2–3) – Matthew makes that clear by writing 'love more than' where Luke just has 'love' (Matthew 10:37).

It's not just family, either – Jesus makes clear that even a person's own life cannot come before the kingdom. They are to live as people who carry around the means of execution – a cross – on their backs (v. 27), because they realise what the alternative is, pictured as a tower which is a folly (vv. 28–30) or a defeated army (vv. 31–32). To follow Jesus costs no less than everything (v. 33).

We may think of people in Jesus' day as mainly relatively poor, and that is true, and thus think Jesus' call is less radical for them than it is for modern westerners with their iPads, computers, mobile phones and many other expensive luxuries. That would be a mistake: loyalty to family was one of the highest cultural values of the day and, in a society where many were poor, the few possessions they had were more highly valued.

In 1956, Jim Elliot and his friends went to take the Christian gospel to the Huaorani people in Ecuador, and were tragically killed by members of the tribe on 8 January 1956. Elliott had written in his journal in October 1948, 'He is no fool who gives what he cannot keep to gain that which he cannot lose', expressing his commitment to serve Jesus at any cost to himself. Elliot left behind his wife Elisabeth and ten-month-old daughter Valerie. Amazingly, Elisabeth, with others, continued the work to share the gospel with the Huaorani with success. Jim and Elisabeth Elliot offer a powerful example of change that can happen when people take Jesus' words seriously.

# 5  Seeking the lost (1): a sheep and a coin

Luke 15:1–10

To an extent, Jesus was crucified because of whom he ate with, for the Jewish leaders regarded his eating with 'tax collectors and sinners' (v. 2) as behaviour not expected of a teacher. Tax collectors collaborated with the pagan Romans, and so were impure by association. Others who did not live as the Pharisees lived, with great concern for keeping even the minutiae of the Jewish law, were 'sinners'.

The Pharisees assume that the company you keep shows your holiness: if you associate with 'sinners', you are polluted by their sinfulness; if you associate with godly people, you are made holy by their holiness. Jesus reverses this assumption: rather than his being polluted by 'sinners', his holiness was contagious and spread to those with him. The three parables in Luke 15 respond to the Pharisees' criticism of Jesus for the company he keeps. Each parable speaks of Jesus' role, and of the people who are acceptable to God.

The lost sheep (vv. 3–7) pictures Jesus as a shepherd caring for a flock. Israel was portrayed as a flock in scripture (e.g. Psalms 77:20; 78:52) and thus God himself was their shepherd (Psalm 80:1). Sometimes the leaders of Israel were pictured as (very bad) shepherds too (e.g. Jeremiah 23:2–3; Ezekiel 34), and a descendant of David (himself a shepherd), the Messiah, would be the true shepherd (Ezekiel 34:23–24).

A hundred sheep would be a large flock, and thus the owner would have subordinates who cared for the sheep. However, in this story, it is not a subordinate whom the owner sends to seek the lost sheep – the owner himself goes (v. 4). The shepherd portrays not only Jesus as the expected Messiah, come to shepherd Israel rightly, but also God, as the 'owner' of Israel, seeking his lost sheep.

It is clear in both parables that God seeks and finds those who respond in repentance – turning from their previous life to a life of following God's way, whether as a shepherd or a woman who has lost a coin from her valuable headdress (vv. 8–10). Jesus does not suggest that people are welcomed without their lives being transformed – for that is what shows they are truly 'found'.

# 6 Seeking the lost (2): two sons

Luke 15:11–32

Jesus continues to respond to the Pharisees' criticism (15:2) with the parable of the two sons. Here, the father loses something far more valuable than a sheep or a coin: his own son, one of only two. Helmut Thielicke calls this story 'the waiting father', a key insight into the parable's meaning.

The three major characters are each significant: the father portrays God's welcoming love; the younger son portrays people who are 'lost' to God; and the older brother portrays the grumpy Pharisees and scribes.

The younger son's request for his share of the inheritance (v. 12) is deeply offensive in this culture – in effect, he is saying that he cannot wait for his father to die. The father's willingness to act in this way is unthinkable – another example of the cartoon-like nature of the parables. When the younger son comes to his senses, he repents, turning to go back to his father and rehearsing his speech (vv. 17–20). His recognition that he has sinned 'against heaven' (v. 18) shows genuine repentance.

The father could stand on his dignity as head of the family. Instead, he both goes to meet his son, rather than waiting for him to arrive, and *runs* out – highly undignified behaviour for a patriarch (v. 20). The father has been looking for him (v. 20) and welcomes him back with celebration and with restoration: he is 'this son *of mine*' (v. 24) – this is the kind of welcome God gives to those who turn back to him.

The older brother is disgusted by the father's welcome and distances himself by speaking of 'this son *of yours*', rather than 'this brother of mine' (v. 30). The older son is just as lost as the younger one had been. He thinks he has been treated unfairly, and so he is unwilling to join the welcome party, even when his father goes out, as he went out to his younger son, and pleads with his son to come in (v. 28) – again, acting in an undignified way.

The father speaks to the older brother as 'My son' (v. 31, NIV), and explains why the celebration was necessary (v. 32). Jesus never completes the story – we never find out whether the older son changed – and that's because the story is an invitation to his audience to change their attitude toward 'sinners' whom Jesus seeks and finds.

# Guidelines: God's welcome and ours

Luke 14—15 offer us a series of pictures of God's welcome of sinners and Jesus' call to discipleship. As often, Luke gets his message across by mixing stories of Jesus' activities with accounts of Jesus' teaching – teaching and action are designed to be mutually interpreting. These chapters raise (at least) two questions worth reflecting on today.

- First, do we see people as God does? Are we in danger of domesticating God as merely the God of acceptable people? The God of Jesus is a welcomer who sees past the outward appearance of people to their real situation and need. More than anything else, Jesus sees that all people are sinners who need repentance (15:7, 10), including the apparently 'clean and sparkly' people who seem to have it all together.

- Second, and in consequence, how wide is our welcome? Here, Jesus heals the man with dropsy (14:1–6), tells a story of welcoming outsiders to a banquet (14:16–24) and responds to criticism of the company he keeps with three stories of seeking and finding the lost (15:1–32).

A fictional story tells of a new pastor of a church who showed up unrecognised to the first service in ragged clothes, dirty and unkempt, and the welcomers sat him at the back of the congregation. He was met with stares and looks of disgust. The church elders then went to the front to introduce the new pastor, and people were shocked when the apparently homeless man walked to the front and read Jesus' words of warning about the need to welcome 'the least of these who are members of my family' (Matthew 25:40). He then asked if they wanted to be disciples of Jesus, and dismissed the service until next week.

The story is based in truth: a number of pastors have lived with homeless people for periods of time, including John Stott, the former rector of All Souls, Langham Place in wealthy west London. The challenge it presents is how we carry out this welcome to sinners and outsiders in our social and cultural setting, both as churches and as individual believers.

---

**FURTHER READING**

Timothy Keller, *The Prodigal God: Recovering the heart of the Christian faith* (Hodder & Stoughton, 2009).

# 1 How to be a crooked manager

Luke 16:1–9

Was Jesus really commending dishonesty by this parable? The crooked household manager, already recognised as such by his master (v. 2), did further wrong to his master by reducing the debts owed to his master (vv. 5–7). And 'the master' commends the manager for this action (v. 8)!

The likely scenario is that the amounts owing to the master were rents in kind for the use of land to grow olives (v. 6) or wheat (v. 7). The master is put in an impossible position when he discovers the changes to the rents: if he reverses the reductions, he would be seen as tight-fisted and mean. So the only option he has is to accept that he would gain a reputation for generosity by his manager's illegal actions, even if he loses out financially. The manager acted brilliantly by putting the master in this dilemma, for it secured the manager's future (v. 4).

So who is speaking the conclusion (vv. 8–9)? Verse 9 is Jesus' comment on the whole story: 'I tell you' reflects Jesus' speech elsewhere (e.g. 11:9; 12:4). However, it seems most likely that at least the first half of verse 8 is spoken by the master in the parable – recall the 'cartoon' nature of parables: even though it is unlikely that a master in the real world would speak so positively of a man who had swindled him, it can happen in 'parable world'.

The master's – and Jesus' – point is that the manager has acted wisely with 'worldly wealth' (NIV) – the Greek represents the Aramaic word for 'possessions' and is morally neutral. Through acting shrewdly, the manager has ensured a welcome into the homes of friends after he leaves his job. Jesus is not commending the manager's dishonest actions, but he is highlighting the need to act wisely with possessions. Jesus' statement that using possessions wisely will lead to his followers being welcomed into 'eternal homes' (v. 9) signals that the 'friends' are 'a heavenly reception committee' (R.T. France). Jesus calls his disciples to use their possessions for heavenly means, for the sake of the kingdom, and to bring good into others' lives. Such behaviour will prepare disciples well for the world to come, which is full of God's generosity and grace.

# 2 Jesus changes the worlds of wealth and 'religion'

**Luke 16:10–18**

Luke here presents some short, sharp sayings of Jesus. The first group is connected by the theme of the right use of wealth (vv. 10–15), and the second group highlights the important transition which Jesus' ministry brings to God's dealings with humanity (vv. 16–18).

Jesus' key question in verses 10–15 is about priorities, for the way people handle their possessions on earth demonstrates whether God will entrust them with spiritual riches (v. 11). Being 'faithful' in the use of possessions means holding them in an open hand, remembering that they are God's gift for the benefit of humanity – they are someone else's property (v. 12) – rather than grasping them with a closed hand and holding on to them for yourself. Disciples must regard their worldly goods as held in trust from God, the generous giver, for 'the earth is the Lord's, and all that is in it' (Psalm 24:1).

'No slave can serve two masters' (v. 13) means that no slave can be entirely owned by two masters at the same time: to put possessions at the centre of our lives, and thus become their slave, is to push God out of the place due to him alone. Thus, following Jesus means giving him the exclusive right to decide what disciples do with their possessions – to act and think any other way is to seek to be a slave of two masters. It is how God sees our lives that matters most (v. 15).

With Jesus' coming, the new age has begun (v. 16), and in this new age there is continuity with the past – even the smallest stroke of a pen will not disappear from the Jewish law (v. 17), including the law about divorce (v. 18). Matthew clarifies that this is because Jesus fulfils the law in his life and ministry, and supremely in his death and resurrection, and this fulfilment produces some continuity and some discontinuity between the law and the new age (see Matthew 5:17–20 with the examples in 5:21–48) – this is a good example where a short saying is the tip of a bigger iceberg of Jesus' teaching, and needs the wider teaching to clarify it.

# 3 How to lose out in the next world

Luke 16:19–31

The way we handle our possessions is a barometer of our spiritual life, according to Jesus. Luke continues to present Jesus' teaching on wealth, here in a hard-hitting parable which reverses the expectations of Jesus' time and culture. Jesus continues speaking to the Pharisees (16:14), and opens a new front in his attack on their love of possessions.

Alongside the common belief that rich people enjoyed God's blessing (e.g. Solomon; see 1 Kings 3:13), Jewish people assumed the rich would be welcomed in the world to come. However, rich people were expected to be generous to poor people by giving alms, as an expression of their faith in God – hence the beggar waited outside the temple's Beautiful Gate (Acts 3:2). It is quite a surprise when the rich man is on the wrong end of the life to come (vv. 23, 26).

The problem is that the rich man ignored the plight of Lazarus (vv. 19–20). Day by day, the rich man passed Lazarus at his gate, in obvious need – the only (temporary) relief Lazarus got was from dogs licking his sores. Yet the rich man never helped Lazarus, and even in the life to come he saw Lazarus as a social inferior – his slave – who could bring water to cool his tongue (v. 24) or be a messenger to his brothers (vv. 27–28). He still doesn't get it!

It's not that the rich man and his brothers don't know better. They hear the scriptures read sabbath by sabbath in the synagogue. So they know of the Mosaic commands to provide for people in poverty (e.g. Leviticus 19:9–10). They hear the prophets' condemnation of rich people who grind poor people into the dirt (e.g. Amos 4:1–3). But they are too busy partying daily (v. 19) to take notice of God's concern for those in poverty.

This is a powerful warning from Jesus that wealth deafens a person to hearing God's word. Jesus challenges wealthy lifestyles which impoverish others, in the first century and today. He signals clearly that life beyond this world is real and that our actions now have consequences then. While we should not necessarily draw conclusions about the specifics of the world to come from this parable – for it is pictorial – the general thrust is clear, and it's not good news for those whose focus is themselves and their own comfort.

# 4 True discipleship

What does discipleship look like? Jesus paints four quick sketches here to show us, as he continues to travel towards his fate in Jerusalem (17:11).

First, discipleship means caring so much for vulnerable fellow-disciples that you avoid causing them to struggle in their discipleship (vv. 1–2). 'These little ones' (v. 2) certainly includes children who follow Jesus (e.g. 9:48), and is also a term used by the gospels for disciples in general (e.g. 10:21, where believers are portrayed as 'infants'; see also Mark 9:42; Matthew 10:42). Jesus values vulnerable people – and he wants his followers to do so to the extent that they adjust their own behaviour to avoid damaging such people.

Second, discipleship means being ready and willing to respond appropriately when a fellow-disciple sins against you (vv. 3–4). Luke is explicit in calling on the offended person to rebuke the offender, in order to evoke repentance, before they forgive. Disciples are not to be doormats – the hard work of forgiveness involves accepting that the other person really has sinned, and naming that as such. This is not to be done in a vindictive or aggressive way, but the offender needs to know what they have done before forgiveness is possible.

Third, discipleship means exercising the faith you have, not the faith you wish you had (vv. 5–6). Jesus rejects the request for greater faith, and instead points the apostles to God's mighty power. Jesus' example of the mulberry tree thrown into the sea could look like an arbitrary act of power – it's a mini cartoon-parable to illustrate the point that small faith can accomplish great things with God.

Finally, discipleship means we must never think we have God in our pocket, that God owes us because of our faithful discipleship (vv. 7–10). A slave (v. 7) simply belongs to their owner – they have no choice about doing what the master says, even if they are tired after a hard day's work. (The NIV is misleading by translating as 'servant', for the story gets its point from the slave's lack of choice.) Jesus is not saying that God is a slave driver, but he is saying that disciples always need to recognise that that even our best efforts fall short of what God deserves (v. 10). 'KOKO' was the slogan of a former generation of Christians: 'Keep on keeping on'!

# 5 An unexpected person responds

**Luke 17:11–19**

Jesus is following the traditional route from Galilee in the north to Jerusalem in the south, travelling along the border between Galilee and Samaria (v. 11), probably planning to cross to the east of the river Jordan and then follow the river south to Jericho, where he would cross back to the west (see 18:35). First-century Jews on pilgrimage to Jerusalem would avoid entering Samaria, for they despised Samaritans: they were half-breeds, descended from Abraham but intermarried with non-Jews; they recognised only the first five books of Jewish scripture (Genesis to Deuteronomy), rather than including the histories, poetic books and prophets; and, worst of all, had their own temple on Mount Gerizim.

It is thus very striking that in dire illness a Samaritan finds himself mixing with Jews. The ten men would be excluded from their respective societies because of leprosy – a word which covered a wide range of skin diseases at this time. They were forced out as a public health measure to prevent leprosy spreading further, and could only return to society when recognised as 'clean' by the priest (for the whole process, see Leviticus 13—14 – part of scripture which Jews and Samaritans shared).

Remarkably, from a Jewish perspective, it is the *Samaritan* who responds to the healing with gratitude, not any of the Jewish men (vv. 15–16). Jesus promises something more to him than healing (v. 19) – his saying plays on the breadth of meaning of 'saved', which can include healing as well as a restored relationship with God.

We've met Samaritans before in Luke, of course. Jesus rejects James and John's hot-headed call to ask God to burn a Samaritan village because they do not welcome Jesus (9:51–56). Jesus tells a parable whose point turns on a Samaritan being the one who helps a needy person (presumably a Jew), rather than apparently pious Jews (a priest or a Levite) (10:29–37). The present story and these other two are found in Luke alone, and are part of Luke's emphasis on Jesus' concern for the outsider and the marginalised – a concern which Jesus' followers will carry through in Acts, as the gospel message reaches out to embrace Samaritans (see Acts 1:8; 8:4–8).

# 6 Kingdom come?

Luke puts the kingdom of God at the heart of Jesus' mission from early on (4:43). God's reign has come near (10:9, 11), and yet disciples pray for its coming (11:2) – and thus it is future too. You can see why the Pharisees asked their question (v. 20a)!

Jesus rejects the assumption that 'the kingdom of God' means a particular event in the future – rather, the reign of God is to be seen among them (vv. 20b–21). KJV's 'the kingdom is *within* you' wrongly suggests that the kingdom is a mystical inner experience or outlook. But Jesus says this to the Pharisees – his opponents – which makes it impossible that he would say the kingdom was within *them*. The word is best translated (with most modern versions) 'among' – the reign of God is present in Jesus among them. If you want to see what God's reign looks like, look at Jesus!

The teaching which follows then makes it clear that there is still a future dimension to the events set in train by Jesus' life and ministry. Luke here presents a unique teaching discourse from Jesus about the days of the Son of Man, with only partial parallels in Matthew 24, and this teaching prepares the way for Jesus' major teaching about the future in relation to the destruction of the Jerusalem temple (Luke 21).

The central figure to this teaching is 'the Son of Man' (vv. 22, 24, 26, 30), a phrase Jesus used to describe himself (as is clear from the warning that the Son of Man must suffer and be rejected, v. 25). Jesus uses this phrase to characterise himself in terms from Daniel 7:13–14, where the prophet speaks of 'one like a son of man' who is brought to God and given universal power and authority. Jesus speaks of a day when he will appear in such a way that everyone will know (v. 24). That day is certainly future – and it requires preparation to be ready.

To alert people to be ready, Jesus uses two biblical pictures of failure to be prepared: the people of Noah's day (vv. 26–27) and the people of Sodom (vv. 28–30). It's all too easy to be so absorbed in present life – eating, drinking, making relationships, making money and working – that God's future becomes so distant that, when it comes, it comes disastrously. You can never out-give God, says Jesus, if you put him at the centre now: lose everything now, and you'll save your life for the future world (v. 33).

# Guidelines: thinking about possessions and money

Jesus' teaching and actions here focus on how his followers handle material goods and money, and in modern western culture they are deeply contemporary and relevant. Like the people of Noah's day or in Sodom (17:26–29), we can easily become wrapped up in this life and making our way in the world, rather than being willing to give time and resources to things which will last into eternity. John White puts it beautifully, using striking images:

*We Christians are visually handicapped. Our perspective is distorted. Bombarded from all sides with false values, living perpetually among people whose goals are material prosperity, security, pleasure, prestige, it is inevitable that we absorb the atmosphere around us until heaven seems remote while the here and now looms large in our thinking. The future comes to mean tomorrow, next week, ten years from now. We are like people looking at curved mirrors in a fun house, but unlike the crowd laughing at the grotesque images, we see the grotesque as normal! It does not amuse us. We base our lives on it.*

*People in Prayer* (IVP, 1978), pp. 131–32

Some years ago, I was at a baptism with a number of family and friends. Following the party afterwards, one couple went to set off home and found that their car had been stolen, stranding them 150 miles from home. Yet, the wife observed, 'in the light of eternity, how important is a car?' This demonstrates the attitude to wealth to which Jesus calls his disciples (e.g. 16:1–9). We hold our possessions lightly, on an open palm, since we have them in trust from God, who owns all things, and we make God's concerns and future the primary influence on our thinking (16:12–13). How do you respond when something which 'belongs' to you is broken or damaged? What's your reaction to things going wrong in your life or the lives of those close to you? Jesus calls his followers to take an eternal view of events.

A church we belonged to has a link with a church in Rwanda, and a team from our church visited our partners (and vice versa). When our team returned from Rwanda, one of the things they remarked on was the amazing generosity of Christians there, who have so much less materially than British people. They were hospitable and generous to the very limit of their means, and sometimes beyond it, and this challenged our team greatly: would they be so willing to give to strangers, even if they were fellow-believers?

# 1 How to pray (1): is God like the unjust judge?

**Luke 18:1–8**

Prayer can be one of the most neglected Christian privileges. It may seem easier to try to fix things ourselves than turn to God; we may neglect to give thanks to God when good things happen. Luke now presents two prayer parables, both unique to this gospel – Luke has a fascination with prayer as a theme.

Luke not only tells us this first parable, but he tells us its point upfront: disciples need to be persistent pray-ers (v. 1). Reading this hard on the heels of Jesus' teaching about being ready for the Son of Man's day (17:20–37), we recognise persistent prayer as a key feature of being prepared for Jesus' return.

The judge only concedes what the widow demands because she keeps asking – and it's exhausting him (v. 5)! The image used is striking: the NIV has 'so that she won't eventually come and attack me!' and that's certainly a possible translation. In the parable-as-cartoon world, the judge is fearful of a black eye from this feisty woman! There's a deep irony in the unjust judge providing justice for the woman for all the wrong reasons.

But is God like the unjust judge? Jesus makes clear that this is a 'how much more' type parable: if even a crooked judge will give justice for purely selfish reasons, how much more will God, the ultimate just judge, give justice to his people who persistently pray to him (vv. 7–8)? The context which Jesus' explanation assumes is persecution, where God's people are desperate for deliverance. In that situation, Jesus promises, God will quickly help his suffering, praying people; that may not mean they will immediately be freed from persecution, as the history of the church shows, but often that they will be sustained to face the tough situation. And further, they will not ultimately lose out on God's final justice.

God knows our situation and loves us, even when the situation is tough. In that situation, Jesus calls us into collaboration with God through persistent prayer – God's ordained means of enabling his people to receive his help and strength in times of trouble.

# 2  How to pray (2): (self-)praise or penitence?

**Luke 18:9–14**

This prayer-parable invites us to consider two different pray-ers going to the Jerusalem temple (v. 10), assembling in the Court of Israel, where Jewish men alone could pray.

Jesus' Jewish audience knew in advance which would be the one Jesus commended: the Pharisee, of course! The Pharisees were godly people who took keeping God's law incredibly seriously. They were students of scripture who applied the law to every part of their lives – even their herb gardens (11:42). Like all prayer in the ancient world, the Pharisee prayed aloud, which meant others would hear. Jesus' hearers would assume that the Pharisee was sincere and correct in describing his own godliness, and in contrasting himself with other 'people of the land', as the Pharisees commonly called other (less godly) Jews (vv. 11–12).

By contrast, Jesus' audience would expect the tax collector to get it in the neck. Tax collectors were the lowest of the low: they collaborated with the hated Roman occupiers to collect the taxes and tolls which the Romans expected. Not only that, but tax collectors were notorious for lining their own pockets by collecting more than the Romans required (see 19:8).

And yet, and yet! Jesus reverses human expectations here – it's not what they've done, but what's in their inner attitudes that's critical. How do they think of God? The Pharisee thinks God welcomes people who are self-congratulatory and rather smug about their relationship with God, and who show that off in public. The tax collector recognises that he deserves nothing at all from God. It's not that he has (as we would say) low self-esteem; he knows that he is a sinner and absolutely needs God's mercy (v. 13). God's radical grace, expressed as the tax collector being 'justified' (v. 14, language more familiar from Paul), means that the key thing to grasp in prayer is that God loves and welcomes genuinely humble people (rather than 'humble braggers') who recognise their need of God – and ultimately, that's all of us!

Why not try praying this: 'God, be merciful to me, a sinner!' (v. 13).

# 3 'Isn't she lovely?'

**Luke 18:15–17**

Modern western societies romanticise babies. We love their promise, their chubby beauty, their potential. On the other hand, we undervalue age and experience: we throw older people on the scrap heap, and look to the young to stimulate and entertain us.

The contrast with first-century culture could not be more total! In all societies known at the time, the wisdom of age and experience were valued. Children, including babies, were at the bottom of the pecking order – they had no rights, no value. It was common in the Greek and Roman worlds for unwanted babies (especially girls) to be 'exposed' – left on the street to die unless someone picked them up.

So when people bring babies to Jesus to touch, it is no surprise that the disciples react negatively (v. 15) – children lack value, save as 'the Israel of the future'. Jesus here turns his culture on its head to teach about God's reign (kingdom). He does not point children to adults to learn what it means to be his followers; rather, Jesus points adults to children – babies! – to see what it means to enter or receive the kingdom of God (vv. 16–17). Jesus teaches two vital themes.

First, the kingdom of God belongs to children and those like children (v. 16). The phrase 'such as these' represents one word in the original, and that word in the New Testament always means 'these [people] and those like them'. In Acts 22:22, the mob in the Jerusalem temple baying for Paul's blood cry, 'Away with *such a fellow*', using the same word as here. The crowd are saying that they want Paul himself, as well as anyone like Paul, done away with. Thus here, Jesus says that the kingdom is the possession of *children and those like them*, with no stated exceptions. That's why, in pastoral ministry, I have no difficulty assuring a parent who has lost a small child that their child is safe with Christ – for the kingdom belongs to *children*, and those like them.

Second, to receive the kingly rule of God necessitates being like a child. This isn't about being innocent (as some today think); rather, it's about the lowly social status and dependence of small children on others. They are *objectively* humble and needy – and receiving God's reign means recognising that is true of us too.

# 4 Wealth and the kingdom of God (1): renunciation

**Luke 18:18–25**

The ruler's question (v. 18) echoes the lawyer's question (10:25), and both make the same assumption: inheriting eternal life requires *doing* something. In both cases, Jesus' response appears conventional within first-century Judaism: he points the ruler to five of the ten commandments (v. 20) and he elicits from the lawyer the two greatest commandments (10:26–27). The law was the way to know God's will and way. In both stories the enquirer pushes deeper, unsatisfied with the conventional answer: here, the ruler claims (no doubt sincerely) that he has kept the five commandments which Jesus lists (v. 21; compare 10:29 and Jesus' parable which follows).

A 'ruler' would be likely to be wealthy – and this one was (v. 23). Jesus' response to him is shocking, for his wealth would normally be seen as a sign of God's blessing in that culture (see notes on 16:19–31). We have heard Jesus warn of the dangers of wealth (e.g. 16:10–15), and teach wealthy people to help those in poverty (e.g. 16:1–9). Now we see Jesus bring these twin themes together in his challenge to the ruler: he must both sell what he has and distribute the proceeds to poor people (v. 22a). But that's not all: the most crucial thing is yet to come.

Jesus calls the man to follow him (v. 22b) – it's insufficient to call Jesus merely, 'Good Teacher' (v. 18). Jesus' call to discipleship to the ruler signals that Jesus is not simply someone to learn from, but someone to follow. If Jesus is truly 'good', then he is truly God (v. 19b) – and to follow God's way means to follow Jesus. The Jewish law prepared the ground for the coming of Jesus and pointed forward to him: now that the reality of God-in-human-form is here, following Jesus is what matters. Interestingly, Luke leaves the ruler's reaction open: Luke doesn't say that the man went away (contrast Mark 10:22) – as with the parable of the two sons, Luke invites his readers to reflect on their response (see notes on 15:11–32).

It would be easy to stop there and miss the challenge of this passage: many assume that the demand to give up his goods was personal to this ruler, that it was a particular issue Jesus identified in his life. But nothing in the text says that: in fact, vv. 24–25 suggest the opposite. Jesus says a similar thing to a wider group in 12:33, and Peter will underline this shortly (18:28). We shall see soon (19:8) that not every disciple gave up everything to follow Jesus – but they did put their riches at Jesus' disposal, and there's the challenge.

# 5 Wealth and the kingdom of God (2): rewards

**Luke 18:26–30**

The conversation between Jesus and the ruler (18:18–25) was not private: others overhead it and were amazed at Jesus' final words (vv. 26–27). Because the conventional wisdom was that riches were a sign of God's blessing, riches were also seen as an 'advance notice' of the likely status of the wealthy in the world to come (recall the surprise of the rich man's torment, 16:23–24). So to suggest that it was hard for wealthy people to enter God's reign (18:24–25) was shocking.

Nevertheless, the question they ask, 'Then who can be saved?' (v. 26), is the right one, and Jesus' answer shines a light on God's power and generous love (v. 27). God can do what people cannot do for, through God's welcome and acceptance of penitent sinners (see Jesus' encounter with Zacchaeus in 19:1–10), God can transform selfish human beings into the people God wants them to be. Jesus' answer points us to discipleship as dependence on God – for that is the one and only way that people become God's people.

Peter immediately opens his mouth and puts his foot in it (v. 28). He's grasped something important: that salvation isn't about wealth, but he's flipped it round and come to the wrong conclusion – that means salvation must be about giving up what you have. So he wants Jesus to know what good disciples he and his colleagues are, for they have given up homes to follow Jesus. Peter is in danger of repeating the ruler's error, of thinking that eternal life can be inherited by *doing* (see 18:18).

I wonder if Jesus sighed when he responded to Peter! Jesus generously overlooks Peter's smug claim, and pushes Peter's thinking on. Remember, Peter, it's all about God doing what people can't (v. 27): that means that the rewards for wholehearted engagement with God's kingdom are out of all proportion (v. 30). 'Many times as much' (NIV) or 'very much more' (NRSV) represent a word found only here in the New Testament which means 'far in excess of a quantity normally expected' (Fred Danker). Yes, there are rewards beyond 'eternal life' for those who faithfully respond to God's call, and they are ludicrously generous – for that's the kind of God who is known in Jesus.

# 6 Who understands Jesus rightly?

Luke 18:31–43

Jesus has long been leading the way to Jerusalem (since 9:51), and will continue to do so (19:28). He now makes explicit why he must go there (vv. 31–33). He again identifies himself as the Son of Man, a figure who suffers before being vindicated by God (see note on 17:20–37), and calls on prophetic scripture as witness to God's painful purposes for him. The focus of Luke's story is narrowing towards the cross, Jesus' supreme act of humble, suffering service to humanity and to God.

The twelve do not understand what Jesus says to them about what is to come (v. 34). That was their reaction when Jesus hinted at the possibility earlier (9:43–45) and, both then and now, something stops them getting it: 'Its meaning was hidden from them' (v. 34, NIV). They do not yet have the spiritual insight, which God alone can give, to see rightly.

Contrast, in a most interesting way, a blind man in Jericho whose spiritual sight is immaculate (vv. 35–43)! Blind people had no other means of support than begging (v. 35), and the pilgrim route to Jerusalem was a good spot to beg. This man moves from being told that 'Jesus *of Nazareth*' is near to identifying Jesus accurately (and at the top of his voice) as 'Son of David' (vv. 38–39). He recognises Jesus as the Messiah, a descendant of King David – the only person in Luke to do so with this title. This recognition emboldens him to ask for 'mercy' (as the ten lepers did in 17:13): an expectation of the Messiah was that he would bring sight to the blind – that's why Jesus answers John the Baptist's question of whether Jesus is 'the one who is to come' by healing (including blind people) and raising the dead (Luke 7:18–22, echoing Isaiah 35:5–6).

Given his earlier insights, the blind man's 'Lord' (v. 41) goes beyond the 'Sir' of polite address – he truly is recognising the remarkable Lord of all who stands before him. In that confidence, he asks for the restoration of his physical sight. His healing moves him from begging, sitting 'by the roadside' (v. 35), to following Jesus and giving glory to God (v. 43). He – a blind man – sees what the twelve don't see, and so he comes to see physically too. Bodily and spiritual sight come together in this beautiful irony.

# Guidelines: Jesus at the centre

Jesus is at the centre of God's purposes in Luke's gospel (as in the other gospels, of course). Luke communicates this by putting Jesus at the centre of the action in story after story. The key question to ask is, 'What's he saying about Jesus?' Here are three answers which emerge from Luke 18:

- Jesus is the full expression of God's generous welcome to those who know they deserve nothing from God. To such people – tax collectors who pray humbly (v. 13), children who are nobodies in their culture (v. 16) or a blind man (v. 38) – Jesus offers the embrace of God which brings healing and forgiveness. When we recognise our own sinfulness and need in relation to God, Jesus stands ready to offer the same welcome to us. Come to him on that basis, and help others to do so!

- Jesus' offer and invitation to us is unconditioned, but not unconditional. It is unconditioned, for it is based on nothing deserving in the recipient – as Paul would have said, it's all God's grace or free gift (e.g. Romans 6:23). But it is not unconditional: it demands a response from the gift-receiver, as all gifts in the ancient world did. Jesus offers no 'cheap grace' which does not transform believers; rather, he points them to the need to relativise their wealth in the light of God's reign (vv. 24–25), and to follow him with praise after the manner of the (healed) blind man (v. 43). Are we ready to pay this price?

- Jesus himself is ready to pay the price of our eternal life (vv. 31–34). He won't hold back from mocking, insults, spitting, flogging and death, because only by travelling that road will he reach the destination of resurrection and new life – for himself and for his people. At this point, Jesus stands alone in understanding his destiny, as the one true Israelite who will walk his path of suffering alone. But he's willing to do that for you and for me, and for millions of others who have walked and will walk with him around this planet over hundreds of years. Doesn't that take your breath away? Doesn't it draw you to humble and delighted worship and praise, just like the blind man (v. 43)?

---

**FURTHER READING**

R.T. France, *Luke* (Teach the Text series) (Baker, 2013).
Tom Wright, *Luke for Everyone* (SPCK, 2001).

# Ruth

## Pauline Hoggarth

One of the most helpful and interesting ways of understanding the Bible is as a still-to-be-completed drama that invites our participation and provides direction for our own 'improvisation' in God's story (N.T. Wright, pp. 88–92). The book of Ruth is part of the third 'act', the story of Israel. In our meditations over the coming week, three questions may keep us on track: first, how do we perceive God's involvement in these events? Secondly, why do the different characters in the story do what they do? And finally, how might their choices inform the way we choose to live? Even if we are familiar with Ruth's story, it will help to read it again at one sitting and with a deliberate openness to discovering it as if for the first time.

The book is anonymous and provokes a wide range of understandings of its purpose. The author may have been a woman (Bauckham, pp. 6–7). She or he certainly provides us with an unusually female perspective on the lives of ordinary people during a lawless period in Israel's history (Ruth 1:1; Judges 21:25). In terms of when the book might have been written, the balance of opinion seems to favour a later, post-exilic date, perhaps to counter the negative view of foreign women expressed in the writings of Ezra and Nehemiah (for example, Nehemiah 13:23–27). Other scholars suggest the purpose of Ruth was to demonstrate the validity of David's kingship as part of God's plans. This would imply an earlier date of composition.

Most intriguingly, several commentators underline the story's subtly subversive nature: for example, 'it insists on the role of women in the Israelite community; on the Moabite origin of its central heroine and of her illustrious descendant, David; as well as on a liberal interpretation of the Torah' (LaCocque, p. 26).

Quotations are from the New Revised Standard Version. Author references are to commentaries in the 'Further Reading' list on page 46.

# 1 When bad things happen…

'Rabbi, who sinned…?' The attitude that prompted the disciples' question to Jesus about the cause of a man's blindness (John 9:1–3) characterises much ancient Christian and Jewish commentary on the opening episode of the book of Ruth. The austere account describes the actions of an ordinary Hebrew family from Judean Bethlehem caught up in a series of catastrophic events over which they have no control. Famine demands survival strategies and difficult decisions. In today's world, they are too often the stuff of heart-breaking media reports. Elimelech, the father of the family (v. 1) – who may or may not have consulted his wife Naomi – chooses to take her and their two sons across the eastern border into famine-free Moab. Maybe he remembered God's encouragement during famine of Isaac's stay among the Philistines, or Jacob's migration to Egypt (Genesis 26:1–3; 46:1–4). His unexplained death and the deaths of his two sons over a period of ten years force new decisions about survival on Naomi, now a vulnerable, alien widow with no protective menfolk (v. 5).

So… who sinned? Why do bad things happen to good people? The emergency migration, the deaths of the men and the childlessness of both sons' marriages are narrated without comment. The author makes no attempt here to provide any 'reason' for the tragedies that overtake this family. (In a contrasting example, Genesis 38:1–10 directly attributes the deaths of Judah's sons to God's judgement on their 'wickedness'.) In the fourth century, St Jerome followed rabbinic tradition in seeking to explain the family's sufferings. This tradition held that Elimelech sinned in leaving Judah and moving to Moab and suggested that the description of the family as 'Ephrathites' (v. 2) implied a degree of aristocracy and wealth that Elimelech hoped somehow to protect by this move. These commentators similarly insist that Mahlon and Chilion also transgressed by marrying Moabite women. True, the relationship between the people of Israel and the Moabites was complex (see Numbers 22 and 25, Judges 11:17–18 and 1 Samuel 22:3–4). But while there were restrictions on relationships, there was apparently no actual prohibition of marriage with a Moabite (Deuteronomy 23:3–6).

At this most hopeless point in the story, Naomi, now merely 'the woman' (v. 5), takes the initiative. And maybe in the news reaching her from Bethlehem (v. 6), we recall Jesus' assurance to his disciples of God at work in the most unlikely circumstances (John 9:3).

## 2  With God against me...

**Ruth 1:8–17**

We inevitably read scripture with a certain worldview that gives more weight to some themes than others. Bauckham (p. 8) points out that western readers often fail to notice that economic security and how to achieve it is at the heart of Ruth's story. It was uppermost in Naomi's mind as the three bereaved women turned their backs on Moab and began to walk westwards. At this point, security was simply something to eat. Presumably the family's food supply in Moab was now cut off with no men to work the land and none of Israel's provision for the poor.

Walking often clarifies our thinking; somewhere on the road, Naomi's mind moved to wider dimensions of security than merely the next meal. (The Hebrew word translated 'security' or 'rest' has the sense of a settled and stress-free place as in the 'still waters' of Psalm 23:2.) In Naomi's understanding, this security must realistically involve remarriage – not now for her (v. 12), but with God's help, still a possibility for Ruth and Orpah among their own people. (Notice how non-territorial Naomi's concept of God is – verses 8–9.) Her pleas to the younger women to secure their future by making the sensible choice – 'Go back... Turn back... Go your way' – are reinforced by her astonishing closing words. Bluntly, she reviews for them the impossibility of any 'levirate' marriages – there will be no brothers for Mahlon and Chilion to provide security for their widows (vv. 11–13).

Naomi is the most complex of all the characters in this story in terms of her relationship with God. She believes that he can bring about blessing in Moab as well as in Judah. At the same time, she believes him to have become her implacable opponent (v. 13b; compare Judges 2:14–15). We will explore her 'bitterness' about God in the next reflection. For now, the younger women must make their choice. Orpah makes her painful but common-sense decision and disappears from the story. Ruth chooses the radical way of unwavering loyalty and carefully considered identification. She chooses to stay with her mother-in-law despite Naomi's attempts to underline the enormity of her choice by comparing it with Orpah's: Ruth would be giving up her community and her gods (v. 15). Like Rahab, another Gentile woman drawn to identify with God's people, Ruth now invokes Israel's God by his divine name, the Lord, who will from now on be hers (v. 17; see also Joshua 2:11–12).

# 3   As it happened...

Ruth 1:18—2:18

The book of Ruth is a brilliantly told story whose power often lies in what the author leaves unspoken and unexplained. Time and again, deliberate ambiguities and omissions confront us, drawing us into the narrative and making us active participants. 'Why? What's going on here?' we keep asking. What lay behind Naomi's strange silence in response to Ruth's outpouring of love and loyalty (1:18)? Did Ruth mean so little to Naomi that she still regarded herself as 'empty' as the two of them returned to Bethlehem (1:21)? And whatever were Ruth's thoughts as she stood by and listened to Naomi's outspoken public complaints about God's harsh dealings with her (1:20–21)?

Whatever she thought and felt, Ruth didn't withdraw into offended silence. She acted on the loyalty she had so movingly promised Naomi, taking the initiative to find food. With Naomi's rather curt permission, she now bravely tests her new community and its values (2:2). Meanwhile, the sudden introduction of a significant new character (2:1) together with the pregnant phrase, 'As it happened...' (2:3) alert us to a turning point in the tale. Alongside the domestic story of hunger, bereavement and complex relationships, and the national story of the uncertain times of the judges, this is a story of God at work. 'As it happened...' signals the mysterious, providential activity of God's Spirit, woven through the lives of ordinary people. Ruth unexpectedly finds herself among Boaz's workers on Boaz's land. (There is an equivalent moment in Esther 6:1.)

In the space of a few days, Ruth witnesses two quite different testimonies to the nature of the God to whom she has pledged allegiance: she listens to Naomi's bitter laments and she relaxes in the warmth of Boaz's detailed kindness. In relation to those laments, maybe Ruth intuitively understood that 'not only is complaint tolerated by God, but it can even be the *proper* stance of a person who takes God seriously' (Peterson, p. 83). And in Boaz,

Ruth witnessed an understanding of God that came off the Torah page (Deuteronomy 10:17–19) to be lived out in his generous and thoughtful welcome of her. What a solace it must have been to this 'foreigner' (v. 10) to hear Boaz's affirmation and realise that his information could only have come from Naomi herself (v. 11)!

# 4  Do not be afraid

**Ruth 2:19—3:15**

Uniquely in scripture, the book of Ruth is mostly dialogue. Of its 85 verses, 55 are direct speech. And nowhere in the story is speech more revealing of the characters' inner processes, and more intriguing, than in the conversations we listen to today.

Naomi's overjoyed response to Ruth's news of her 'chance' encounter with Boaz is the central turning point of the story. The passive, embittered widow can finally acknowledge that the Lord's faithful loving-kindness, his *hesed*, has in truth never abandoned her family, living or dead – and now she includes Ruth in that family! Boaz 'is a relative of *ours*, one of *our* nearest kin' (2:20), a 'redeemer' kinsman with the right and responsibility to help out a family member in financial straits (Leviticus 25:25–28). But there is already a note of caution in Naomi's words; Boaz may not be the only one with that status.

The continuing conversation between the two women is interestingly ambiguous. Boaz had asked Ruth to keep close to his female workers (2:8). Ruth reports his instructions to Naomi in broader terms (2:21) that may reflect Moabite openness or maybe her anxiety about how to meet a man in this new community – maybe among Boaz's male workers? Whatever motivates Ruth, she now quietly follows Naomi's advice. With the harvest ending, the dangers recede for Ruth as an unprotected outsider, but her future remains discouragingly unresolved (2:23).

Energised by Ruth's news, Naomi once more takes the initiative. And what a risky initiative! She must engineer an opportunity for Ruth to be alone with Boaz so that he can make his intentions clear to her (3:4). Now nothing is left to chance. Perfume and her best outfit will make clear to Boaz that Ruth is open to leaving widowhood behind (3:3). 'All that you tell me I will do,' Ruth assures Naomi (3:5). In the event, she bravely and humbly speaks her own words and in tactful terms asks Boaz for marriage, carefully reminding him of his redeemer kinsman status that will also benefit Naomi (3:9). (The image of the protective cloak in this verse may deliberately echo Boaz's words about God's protective 'wings' in 2:12; see also Ezekiel 16:8.)

Boaz's touching response to Ruth is pure delight (3:10). From now on, his energies will be directed at freeing Ruth from all fear: fear of gossip (3:14), of hunger (3:15) and of insecurity (3:13).

# 5 Redeemed

Ruth 3:16—4:12

We can imagine Naomi pacing the floor as she waits for Ruth's return from the threshing floor. Her first urgent question is the same as Boaz's to Ruth during the night (3:9): 'Who are you?' Clearly Naomi recognises Ruth, her 'daughter'; her question now is about a possibly – hopefully – changed identity following the encounter with Boaz: from widow to betrothed. Boaz's extravagant gift of grain for Naomi is a deeply symbolic sign of hope, another signal of the transformation of Naomi's emptiness (3:17) and of Ruth's future security.

It is not easy to understand the legal process that Boaz steered at the town gate, and the reasons for it. If Naomi had access to some family land in Bethlehem, why is there so much emphasis in the story on her poverty? Under Jewish law, widows did not inherit their husbands' or sons' property, so what right did Naomi have to sell her husband's land? Maybe she had received the land as a dowry, and as a widow took ownership of it again. However we understand the introduction of this new element, the land is useless to Naomi without menfolk or employees to work it. Boaz reports her wish to sell to someone within her clan as the law required (see Leviticus 25:23–25).

Boaz seems relaxed, not summoning the anonymous second kinsman redeemer, but offering a friendly invitation when he happens to come by (4:1), and only then requesting the presence of the community elders as witnesses. The second kinsman's calm agreement to buy the land (4:4) turns into a hasty withdrawal as Boaz informs him of conditions. Here there is even more scholarly controversy, focusing on the translation of 'you acquire' in verse 5. The Hebrew can be translated either as 'you must acquire/marry Ruth' or 'I acquire/marry Ruth.' Only the second interpretation makes sense of the kinsman's reaction as he realises that it would be Elimelech's family, through Boaz and Ruth, who would inherit this land (4:6).

This cliffhanger of a scene is resolved with the ceremonial transfer of a sandal to ratify the transaction (compare Deuteronomy 25:9), Boaz's bold 'mission statement' (4:10) and the community's joyful vision of the home that Boaz and Ruth will make together and the children God will bring (4:11–12).

# 6  To Naomi, a son

Ruth 4:13–22

Just when we would expect to hear Ruth and Naomi joyfully welcoming the birth of Ruth's baby, we find them strangely silent. Maybe silence is the appropriate response to finding yourself caught up in God's mysterious purposes. Ruth's marriage to Mahlon had been childless; now she is pregnant. The deliberate reference to God's intervention (v. 13) echoes the 'impossible' birth of Isaac (Genesis 21:1–7). The Lord's long-term purpose of bringing blessing to all the families of earth (Genesis 12:1–3) has now drawn into it an alien Gentile woman to provide the next link in the chain.

Once again, we find ourselves imagining Ruth's thoughts as the chorus of neighbourhood women seems to sideline her to address Naomi (vv. 14–15). Even the name they give the baby – Obed – seems to reflect their focus on their elderly clanswoman and the transformation in her circumstances that they have witnessed. Obed means 'worker', one who will be able to work the newly redeemed land. The village women are not thinking about the future family line; they 'are solely interested in the child because he will resolve the emptiness of Naomi's life' (McKeown, p. 68). There may be a gentle reproof to Naomi in the women's affirmation of Ruth as 'more to you than seven sons' (v. 15). Naomi had conformed to the norms of her patriarchal society, valuing men – her sons and husband – over women (1:8–13). The narrative doesn't record a single direct word of appreciation from Naomi to Ruth. But, over the months of the barley harvest, the village women had watched Ruth hard at work in the fields to provide for Naomi. Now they seem to want her to know how much the community values her – and maybe they are suggesting it's time Naomi acknowledged her worth to her.

The genealogy that closes the book of Ruth covers ten generations. Some commentators believe these closing verses were a later addition, while others understand them to be in deliberate narrative balance with the ten years in Moab that open the story (1:4). A story that began in ten years of grief and emptiness closes with a ten-generation genealogy of hope and promise which will be expanded even more hopefully in Matthew to include three 'outsider' women: Tamar, Rahab and Ruth (Matthew 1:1–6) and conclude in the birth of Jesus the Messiah.

## Guidelines

- 'So the book of Ruth... shows us that salvation history is continuous and not intermittent... It shows us that those whom God saves by signs and wonders... he continues to save by his providential workings in their day-to-day lives, and that his kindness (*hesed*), by which Israel is built up, is to be found not only in great national deliverances, but in the way his covenant people treat one another on a daily basis. It is micro, as opposed to macro, salvation history' (Barry G. Webb, p. 53). In what ways do you understand Christians' kind and compassionate treatment of one another and of others as 'micro salvation history'?

- 'A story told with pathos, humour or drama opens the imagination and invites readers and hearers to imagine themselves in similar situations, offering new insights about God and human beings which enable them then to order their own lives more wisely' (N.T. Wright, pp. 19–20). In what ways have you discovered new insights in the story of Ruth and how might you experience them shaping your decisions and actions?

- At the time of writing these reflections, the 'Me Too' campaign has high-lighted abuse of power in relationships between men and women. How might the account of Boaz's behaviour towards Ruth and Naomi, and their behaviour to him, contribute to the debates about male/female relationships?

- 'The alien who resides with you in your land shall be to you as the citizen among you; you shall love the alien as yourself, for you were aliens in the land of Egypt' (Leviticus 19:34). Meditate on these demanding words and turn them into prayer for the 'aliens' in your community and those who support them.

## FURTHER READING

Richard Bauckham, *Is the Bible Male? The book of Ruth and biblical narrative* (Grove Books, 1996).

André LaCoque, *Ruth: A continental commentary* (Augsburg Fortress, 2004).

James McKeown, *Ruth* (Eerdmans, 2015).

Eugene H. Peterson, *Five Smooth Stones for Pastoral Work* (John Knox Press, 1980).

Barry G. Webb, *Five Festal Garments: Christian reflections on the Song of Songs, Ruth, Lamentations, Ecclesiastes and Esther* (IVP, 2000).

N.T. Wright, *Scripture and the Authority of God* (SPCK, 2005).

# Genesis 12—36

Brian Howell

The Old Testament story of God's sustained intervention in the world begins with 'Father Abraham'. The father of countless tribes, Abraham is truly a watershed in the history of human culture, belief and ethnicity. However, his story as told in Genesis serves as a study in the nature of God's relation with people, his plan of salvation for them and the nature of biblical faith. In this selection of notes, we chose to highlight key episodes in the lives of the patriarchs and matriarchs which develop not only their character but illuminate the character and nature of divine interaction in the world.

Perhaps what is so scandalous about Abraham is that of his particularity. God chose this man to work through, promised him his blessings, fought for him and used both him and his descendant(s) as his preferred conduit to bless and rescue the world. But this choice was not due to anything Abraham had done or deserved. In fact, several times Abraham seems to nearly sabotage the entire mission. It is this scandal of particularity that makes the Bible transcend the calculations of philosophy – of what a perfect being should be and do. Here, we find the rather messy story of what such a being actually did – the 'actual' taking precedence over the 'ideal'.

It is this mystery of God's choice which both humbles and enlightens us. We, quite naturally, often think he ought to have used someone more honest, more confident, less war-like, but he did not. And yet, when we feel he will only use those better than ourselves, he again chooses otherwise.

But, we also see *how* God works with these imperfect characters. All is not revealed at once, but in due time and context. Though he makes promises of protection and blessing while they are still quite broken characters, he is not content to leave them as they are. Though Jacob does experience God's hedge about him and indeed his favour upon his work, he must engage with God on the deepest level – something from which no one escapes unchanged – before he can finally come home.

Quotations are from the New American Standard Bible.

# 1 Enter Abram

**Genesis 11:27—12:3**

Abram's story begins following the *toledot* ('these are the generations of...') formula. This occurs ten times in Genesis and structures all the narratives following creation, underscoring the playing out of the mandate to 'be fruitful and multiply'. Oddly enough, in 11:27, Terah is not the focus of the following stories. Rather, the focus of each section following the formula is on the son or sons of the one named; in this case, Abram.

When we first encounter them, our focal family is already on the move. Terah relocates his family out of the 'cradle of civilisation' at Ur (near modern Bosra in Iraq) towards the land of Canaan, but they only make it as far as Haran, where we are told they 'settled' (v. 31). The implication of this double entendre is not only that they didn't get to where they were meant to be, but perhaps that they allowed themselves to get too comfortable before their journey was complete. It is upon the death of Abram's father that God now intervenes.

Set against the downward spiral of humanity presented in the 'proto-history' (Genesis 1—11), this intervention signals God's intentions to reverse the trajectory of moral decay and increasingly pointed human rejection of their Creator. Even after the worldwide flood of Genesis 6—9, humanity is seen as collectively bent on building their own legacy apart from God (Genesis 11).

Enter our hero and heroine. However, along with their introduction in 11:29-30, one of the central problems of Genesis is introduced: infertility. Not only is this a very personal problem for Abram and Sarai, but it is also the first mention of human incapacity to fulfil the creation mandate. Unable to build a family, they alone were faced with the impossibility of following the rest of their race in their preoccupation with their own immortality, whether through forbidden fruit opening their eyes like God's, heaven-breaching towers or progeny with divine beings (compare 6:1–4).

However, this hardship turns out to be a blessing in disguise. When God promises Abram 'to make his name great', this is no kind gesture but an answer to the failed attempts of humanity to make a name for themselves apart from their Creator (compare 11:4). Only here, it is God who will be making Abram a name, not Abram himself.

# 2 The blessing of Abra(ha)m

In verse 1, we find God ordering Abram to 'Go, for yourself' (*lek-leka*). Especially in a culture where one's identity, financial security and legal justice were wrapped up in one's family and community, this command to strike out on his own would seem very disorienting. As Abram has already left his homeland, this is a confirmation that he is to continue in his trajectory away from the centre of a civilisation bent away from God. Not only this, but he is also to go away from his immediate family. He is not to 'settle' as they have but to proceed, not to what looks good or is comfortable or to what others think is best, but to a place where God directs him.

We have here a radically different decision-making process. No longer is it based on human reasoning and culturally informed values, but upon a voice – a revelation – that breaks into human history from the outside. Though the promise is conditional upon Abram's obedience, it is overwhelmingly weighted towards God's commitment to Abram. If Abram but follows, God will give him the moon!

The blessing is compound, beginning with the element of land. This is not only a place to live, but an end to the transient life that Abram's obedience initially entails. God does not command him to live a nomadic life forever.

Making Abram a great nation answers the problem of infertility we are first confronted with, but it goes beyond simply granting Abram offspring. It speaks of his significance, for not only will Abram's lineage and heirs continue, they will thrive and become one of the significant landed political communities in the world.

Finally, Abram will be blessed. This means not only that Abraham's name will be used as a blessing, 'May you be [blessed] like Abraham' (see Genesis 28:4) but also that he will be a conduit of blessing. As Wenham has pointed out, this is most likely the middle sense (G. Wenham, *Genesis 1–15*, p. 277). Abram won't just be blessed (passive) or bless himself (reflexive), but others will 'find blessing' in him. That is, it is not necessarily anything Abram will do that blesses them, but who he is and how they relate to him and his descendants which will determine whether they find themselves blessed.

# 3 God of purity

It is somewhat shocking that Abram, upon hearing that Canaan is the 'land which I will show you' (12:1), continues to Egypt. Even more disconcerting is the collusion with his wife to pass her off as his sister to avoid himself being killed because of her great beauty. She is about 65, but this is actually only midlife (compare 23:1). Notably, her formidable pulchritude is conspicuously absent in the parallel passage in Genesis 20 where she is 99.

Abram's ruse is confusing on the surface. Why does he think he will survive the Egyptian's desire if he calls Sarai his blood relative? We learn later that Abram's lie in verse 13 is actually only a half-truth – she is the 'daughter of [Abram's] father' (20:12), though this could mean that she is an adopted sister, not merely a step-sister. Sarna has brought up some Hurrian texts that appear to open the possibility that one could make one's wife their adopted sister; however, these are unclear and don't seem to solve the problem. A more likely scenario is presented by Cassuto, following medieval commentators who suggest that, as with Laban and Rebekah, or Dinah and her brothers, a brother could at least fend off a sister's suitors (Wenham, *Genesis 1–15*, p. 288).

But what of Pharaoh? He seems to conduct himself more uprightly than Abram. Though Pharaoh acted in ignorance, neither this nor lack of intent exonerates one in the Old Testament. One is always responsible for one's actions, in this case adultery, even if they are not part of God's covenantal family. Notably, Pharaoh acts very similarly to God in Genesis 3, where he asks the same question of Abram that God did of Eve – 'What have you done?' (v. 18) – and likewise sends Abram out of the country (compare 3:23). Due to these parallels with the garden of Eden, it seems that Pharaoh's responses to Abram function not only to share his personal frustration with Abram, but to raise deeper questions for both the patriarch and those who find themselves his descendants. Why would the patriarch put those outside the covenant in danger from God's curse (12:3) through attempts at *self*-preservation? This attitude not only displays a lack of faith in his covenant partner, but also puts others at risk.

# 4 Between two altars

Thrust out of Egypt, God again demonstrates to Abram the nature of his promises. Superseding Abram's attempts to preserve himself from famine and foreigners, God now shows Abram that his blessings override even the quarrels of his kinsmen.

Just as Abram had left the land of promise in the previous chapter, so here he appears to leave the land by leaving his place of residence up to his nephew. He does this, disregarding the fact that that location was key to both the obedience go 'to a land which I will show you' and the promise of the divine blessings (12:1–3).

But there is something else going on here. Abram is demonstrating a high value in the ancient Near East – that of hospitality. Abram shows deference to Lot – whom he had brought along on this journey and who is a member of his own (extended) house. This sort of treatment, both of guests and kinsman, will contrast greatly with later patriarchs, especially Jacob, who, initially at least, uses his own people to get ahead and achieve a 'blessing' (27:36). Despite Abram's *display* of hospitality towards Lot, something he was afraid was lacking in Egypt, God again demonstrates that his promise is not dependent upon Abram's looking out for himself. Whereas Abram offers Lot the choice to the right or left, God promises Abram all four points of the compass (v. 14). This promise is more definite than that in chapter 12, for it is now 'all the land which you see', which is promised to both his descendants and himself and is done so 'forever' (v. 15).

Initially, in verses 3–4, we find Abram relocating the altar he had built in 12:8. As Wenham says, 'The narrator is surely suggesting that Abram is trying to recapture his previous experience of God' (*Genesis 1–15*, p. 296). However, this previous encounter will not be his last, making his faith solely an exercise in memory and sentiment. God renews his promise to Abram, reaffirming its ongoing legitimacy and honing its terms, making them a bit more concrete. Thus, the promise theme becomes one not only of the trust in what God has done, but of how he is refining and developing the trajectory of his will, blessing and people.

# 5 God Most High

This chapter mentions a triplet of battles involving the kings of the east, not only versus the western kings, but also versus the Dead Sea kings, and finally versus Abram. Abram is here labelled a 'Hebrew'. This designation (*habiru*) is only used by foreigners speaking of the Hebrews, and in non-biblical texts indicated someone on the fringes of society, sometimes a mercenary. This accurately describes Abram, who is still sojourning in a land not yet his own.

The prowess of Chedorlaomer, who has apparently become the leader of the coalition by the second battle, serves to make Abram's triumph all the more significant. This is a powerful, militarily savvy king who is taken out by Abram's small band, similar to Gideon's upset of the Midianites (Judges 7:7).

Despite the king of Sodom greatly benefiting from Abram's martial blessing, he was only interested in getting his people back (v. 21). Though the spoils would have been Abram's by right, and some appreciation due, the king of Sodom remains shameless. Though Abram is concerned that the king of Sodom cannot brag about making him rich, impugning his motives (vv. 22–24), he was not so concerned about plundering the Egyptian king through his misrepresentations about Sarai being his wife. This is no maturing of his character, as he repeats his wife-sister scheme again in Genesis 20. Rather, we find that Abram is not after sordid gain, but self-preservation and that of his (currently perceived) heir.

However, the King of Salem sees something different. He too would have benefited from Abram's military exploits, but he sees God's hand on him. Acting as both king and priest (common in the ancient Near East), instead of taking, he gives a blessing to Abram by 'El 'Elyon, or 'God Most High' (vv. 18–20). As king of Salem (presumably Jerusalem) and a Canaanite, this epitaph probably referred to the high deity of the Canaanite pantheon, 'El. An editor connects this with Yahweh, or the Lord, so the readers see that Abram wasn't worshipping some Canaanite deity. (We know this was added later because God's covenant name was not revealed until Moses; see Exodus 6:3.) Rather, just as the apostle Paul later made 'the unknown god' known as Jesus, so here 'the Most High', the creator of heaven and earth – a compound term not used in Canaanite texts – is now identified as the God of Israel.

# 6  A God of a covenant people

As part of this new covenant, God's words to Abram in this pivotal chapter resound with those of Melchizedek. God promises to be Abram's shield (*magen*) just as the Canaanite priest-king praised the Most High for delivering (14:20, *miggen*) Abram. However, Abram's complaint in response to God's command not to fear (v. 1) still seems a bit faithless. But, upon closer inspection, it too seeks the fulfilment of what God had promised earlier in terms of progeny and making Abram a great nation. He is neither despairing of nor disparaging God's promise, but simply holding him to it. In verse 4, again the promise is made more specific – Abram's heirs will come from his own body.

It is significant that Abram's faith is counted as righteousness. Faith does not simply produce it but stands in place of it. It seems to be made up of two elements – that of trust in God's promises and that of obedient action in response to his commands.

Later, we find an odd covenant-sealing practice. Abram is seen shooing birds away from the sacrifices he has split in half. The sacrifice made by splitting the animals and having the covenant parties walk between them is typically understood to be a self-directed curse, meaning something to the effect of: 'May I become like these animals if I do not hold up my part of this covenant.' Up until now, God's covenant with Abram had been conditioned on his obedient response. Now, having found Abram faithful, he has counted this as righteousness or being right with God, and he cements the promise – now without condition. God is the only party who walks between the carcasses, and thus the only one taking a now unilateral oath.

God not only promises to be the shield Melchizedek proclaimed, but he will be the ally the Amorites formerly were (compare 14:13; see Bruce K. Waltke, *Genesis: A commentary*, p. 240). In fact, there is a prophecy in verse 16 in which the sin of the Amorites is said not to be complete. There is no indication that Abram's current allies were guilty of any indiscretions, but God knew the depraved place the Amorites were heading, and needed to break Abram away from such influences.

# Guidelines

- Abram and Sarai must surely have felt their infertility was a curse – especially in a culture that valued childbirth so highly. What 'curses' do we feel are in our lives? What flipsides might these coins have – what unique perspectives do they give us, or warped cultural values might they shield us from?

- How flexible are we? The things we 'cannot live without' are quite often the idols that both anchor and weigh us down. If God is on a mission, as he certainly was with Abram, then it may be that the key quality of our life of faith is an openness, an un-tied-down-ness, to be able to go with him. What aspects of your life do you feel you cannot live without?

- Abram models for us at least two approaches to our encounters with God. When in need of one's spiritual bearings, it is often helpful to go back to where we encountered God in the past. This reminds us of the reality of his work in our lives and reorients us to where we saw him heading last. If he hasn't given us a new direction, it is best to continue to do what we last sensed from him. However, Abram also demonstrates that the past promises of God can be made new – either more specific or confirmed in their continuing relevance or, sometimes, with corrective lenses. That is, the way we once interpreted God's signs and words may no longer be valid, or we may have misinterpreted them all along.

- How do we treat those who are not of our tradition? True worshippers of God may not look very much like us, and even more similar to those we might consider non-believers. Yet, throughout the Bible, we find those who acknowledge God in the strangest places. How do we respond when we are blessed by those we least expect?

- Finally, like Abram, do we hold God to his promises? There are certainly parts of our journey with God that fall upon our own shoulders, but how much do we require of him? Faith is ultimately in the one we cannot see and, crucially, this makes him the bearer of the weight of fulfilling the promise. Abram could be obedient, but he could not determine where God would lead or when he would grant fertility.

# 1 A God who sees (1)

Genesis 16 is often viewed as a story about how Sarai tried to fulfil God's promise of a child by taking matters into her own hands. However, this plotline is resolved by verse 6, with Sarai not even mentioned in the rest of the chapter.

There are several things about this story that indicate it is more than meets the eye. Initially, we note the list of Hagar's titles. She is first introduced as an Egyptian slave, likely obtained through Abram and Sarai's jaunt there in Genesis 12. Though she begins as Sarai's handmaid (*shiphchah*), she is elevated to Abram's wife (v. 3), only to be demoted back down to maid. She then hits bottom as she becomes the lowest ranking member of society – a runaway, female slave. The rise and fall of Hagar as seen in her titles alerts us to one of the key issues of the chapter, which culminates in her giving a name to God – the only character in all of scripture to do so.

It is at this lowest of points that the angel finds Hagar and asks where she is going. Though she is clearly heading home to Egypt (v. 7), her answer displays her mental state: she is heading not *to* somewhere, but *from* – she is fleeing her mistress. We are shocked to find our hero couple the perpetrators of such abuse. Why do they give such ill treatment to this maid?

Sarai seems to have blamed Abram for her maid's air of superiority. She is likely wondering whether or not Abram gave his new 'wife' the idea that she now outranked his first one. After all, Hagar was going to bear him a child. Abram responds, saying, 'Your maid is in your power,' thereby placing her back under Sarai in the chain of command and denying any culpability for the maid's notions of grandeur. However, this move allows Sarai to take out her indignation on her maid, so harshly that she runs away.

The angel who finds her does something that Abram and Sarai never did – use Hagar's name. This demonstrates God's personal knowledge of and care for Hagar, despite the fact that the couple through whom God will bless the nations are anything but a blessing to Hagar.

# 2  A God who sees (2)

The fact that the angel of the Lord cares for Hagar raises the question of why he would send her back to what is sure to be more abuse. The answer lies in the greater context – the Abrahamic blessing. When Hagar became pregnant, Sarai became 'despised' (v. 4, *qalal*) in her sight. This is the same verb in Genesis 12:3 which states that those who even 'despise' (*qalal*) Abram, God will curse (*'arar*). The one who merely looks down on Abram, God will respond to in a much harsher way. Hagar has essentially put herself on the wrong side not of history, but of God's favour.

Hence, if Hagar is to receive God's blessing, she must be rightly related to the couple whom he has chosen as his conduit of blessing. By returning and humbling herself before Sarai, she is treating this conduit with the appropriate respect, regardless of the treatment she receives. A confirmation of this key connection is that in Genesis 12:3, all the families (*mishpechah*) of the earth will find blessing in Abram (and by extension, Sarai). By remaining Sarai's *shephchah* (same root as 'families'), Hagar indeed finds blessing, not from her mistress, but from her God, as her son will become the head of twelve princes (Genesis 17:20), and four times she is associated with Abram at the end of chapter 16.

Although her promised son will be named Ishmael, or 'God hears', she responds, 'You are a God who sees' (v. 13). 'Hearing' seems to refer to the anguish she endured at the hands of her mistress. But for her, this is more than pain – it is a great fall. Having been raised to the status of wife – and one with great honour in bearing a child, she has sunk to the lowest status in society. So why 'God sees?' Though the rest of verse 13 is a tricky translation, it should be rendered, 'Now I have truly seen according to the One Who Sees Me.' In other words, she now sees herself not according to the conventions of society, but according to how God sees her – full of promise and worth. It is this which explains how a woman who previously had tried to climb the social ladder only to fail miserably could return not only to harsh treatment, but also to no change in status. She received her worth from a new place.

# 3  God of refining promises

The reiteration and honing of God's promise falls on the heels of the Hagar episode. Up until this point, it has been unclear who would be Abram's heir. Would it be his nephew Lot, or the highest-ranking servant in his house (Eliezar)? Here, it looks like it will be Ishmael, who, though born to a concubine, was in the eyes of the ancient Near East a legitimate heir. The 18th century BC Mesopotamian King Hammurabi's law code deals with such 'surrogate' pregnancies, insisting that the firstborn, whether of the slave girl or the primary wife, should retain the lion's share of the inheritance. In fact, the child of the slave girl was considered to be that of the primary wife.

So when God again speaks to Abram, part of his purpose is to demonstrate that the heir is to be born of Abram's primary wife, Sarai. It is interesting that Abram's seemingly faithless petition, 'Oh that Ishmael might live before You!' (v. 18) is both ignored and heard. God has a plan – to come through with his promise in his own way and time – which remains unaltered in the face of Abram's request. But God still hears Abram and grants his misguided but good-hearted wish – his prayers are still significant.

It is also interesting that God changes the name of Abram to Abraham. Names were seen to reflect the character or destiny of the person who bore them. His first name, Abram, must have seemed a cruel joke to the patriarch, as 'exalted father' must have been salt in the wound of a childless man. However, after Ishmael is born, Abram could take refuge in his fatherhood, feeling he had indeed lived up to his name. But God, who would 'exalt' this father, would do so through a second child. Hence, the name no longer reflected what God intended to do through him. Rather, Abraham, 'father of many', covers both the fact that more than one nation would issue from him, but also that he would be looked to by many as the father of their own faith, regardless of their lineage.

# 4 God of justice

In what appears like haggling, Abraham appeals to God to save Sodom for the sake of 50 righteous, working him down until he reaches ten. This actually wasn't bartering, as then Abraham would be trying to push the price up, not down, and truly he had nothing to bargain with – to meet God in the middle.

If Abraham is not actually changing God's mind about how many righteous will save the city, what is going on? The key is found in God's self-talk. Here we get a glimpse into God's thought process – why does he deem it necessary to tell Abraham what he is about to do? Verse 19 reveals a condition to God's promise to making him a great nation and conduit of blessing to the nations – justice and righteousness. Abraham must teach his descendants this 'way of the Lord' in order for the promise to come about. Justice and righteousness are key to God's blessing.

In the prophets, these two terms are a *hendiadys* – one idea expressed in two words, much like Shakespeare's 'sound and fury' (*Macbeth*, Act 5, Scene 5). Justice has to do with upholding the law. It gives people what they deserve for their actions. But righteousness is a relational term – akin to doing right by or being right with someone. The two together push the concept past mere justice. That is, to simply do justice can be cold-hearted. However, to show mercy can end up eroding the law itself, rendering it toothless and banal. To combine the two is not simply to abide by the law, but champion those who don't get a fair shake in court. It is to stand up against unjust laws or their unfair implementation. It is in this sense that Abraham is being taught, almost Socratically, by God about righteousness and justice.

It is a forgone conclusion that God will bring justice against the Sodomites. It is both the righteous and righteousness that are at stake (v. 25). As with his battles in chapter 14, it is his nephew on whose behalf Abraham seeks the stay of punishment. But in order for Abraham to be a blessing to all nations (v. 18–19), God is teaching him to champion others, rather than letting the brimstone fall where it may.

# 5 God of judgement

The two men sent to Sodom turn out to be angels, but why would God send them down there? In 18:21, it seems to indicate that God does not know what the Sodomites have done and is checking the situation out. Actually, there is evidence he does know. In 13:13, there is an outright statement about the cities' exceeding wickedness, labelling them 'sinners against the Lord'. Genesis 18:17 indicates God already knows what he is going to do to Sodom, conducting an internal deliberation about whether or not to tell Abraham. Furthermore, in 18:20, God pronounces Sodom's sin as 'exceedingly grave'.

It turns out that these two angels were sent, not to gain knowledge of Sodom's sin, but to present proof of it. In Hebrew law, a fact must be established on the testimony of two witnesses (Deuteronomy 17:6–7; 19:15). Hence, they are essentially providing legally acceptable proof, both to Abraham and to the Sodomites themselves, that God knows the evil of their deeds.

In addition to witness and judgement, the angels seek to remove the only ones in the city who haven't been fully corrupted. That this was a mission of mercy towards Lot's family, and not a fact-finding mission, is confirmed in 19:13, when the men tell Lot that 'the Lord has sent us to destroy [the city]'.

There has been some debate over the nature of the Sodomites' sin in light of the homoerotic attack upon the men sent to get Lot. Indeed, this is where the act of sodomy gets its name. However, in Ezekiel 16:49–50, something more is indicated. In contrast with both Abraham and Lot, the Sodomites are depicted as utterly devoid of hospitality. They not only didn't care for those in need, but they violated the protection a guest was traditionally extended when they came under someone's roof. The 'abominations' spring up due to the absence of hospitality, which Jude 6–7 seems to take as referring to the angelic/human unions of Genesis 6:1–4. Thus, going 'after strange flesh' (Jude 7) could be describing the desire of the Sodomites to cross such human/divine boundaries, as the men sent to Sodom were indeed angels. In any case, we are dealing with a sin far beyond homosexual rape, as the book of Hebrews warns: 'Do not neglect to show hospitality to strangers, for by this some have entertained angels without knowing it' (Hebrews 13:2).

# 6 No laughing matter

In verse 6, Sarah says that, 'God has made laughter for me; everyone who hears will laugh with me.' Indeed, this was a reminder of what had happened back in 18:12–15, where she herself had laughed at God for predicting she would have a child in her old age.

Although the name Isaac meant laughter, not all found this very funny. Seeing the child of the slave woman – notably not named, emphasising his lineage – Sarah demands to throw him out. Many translations have Ishmael 'mocking', though the object of this scorn remains unstated – presumably Isaac. However, the verb here is the same one Sarah used in verse 6 – *tsachaq* – and from which we get the name Isaac – 'to laugh'. Though it is in the intensive here, this does not always have a negative connotation – as Isaac later is caught 'caressing' (or 'playing') with his wife Rebekah (26:8). Ishmael could simply have been joking around or playing with the new baby. The problem may not lie in the object of the boy's (he is now around 13) laughter or playfulness, but in Sarah's statement – 'laugh *with me*'. A surrogate child, if first-born, would have the inheritance rights of the firstborn, even over the son of the primary wife. Thus, Sarah does not want Ishmael to laugh with her, as his very presence is a threat to the fulfilment of the promise she had – that the heirs to God's promise would come through her own child. Hence, she wants Ishmael sent away.

Abraham, though troubled by this, seems cold, only giving them a skin of water and some bread, rather than the inheritance of a very rich man. However, he is giving her more than some tawdry staples. In effect, he gives her an act of manumission – her freedom. Though she is no longer part of his house, which included servants and the children born to his wives, she is now a free woman and her son will be a free man as well. This sets in motion not only the fulfilment of the promises concerning Isaac, but those about Ishmael as well. He will not be known as a slave, but as his own man – free to become the prince he is destined to be.

# Guidelines

- Hagar desires respect. Initially, she saw that as a function of her status in society, both in terms of being married and then in having children. Though these values aren't as stressed today, they still remain primary drivers for many. But God wanted her to see that she had value that society would never recognise, especially knowing her status would always be very much in flux. What positions, accomplishments, or acquaintances do we attach our feelings of worth to? How does God see us differently?

- In Hagar's struggle to climb the social ladder, she ends up looking down on someone God has blessed. When have we disrespected those in authority over us, justifying our stance by pointing out their flaws? God is clear about the respect we need to show those he has placed over us and how crucial this is for our own blessing.

- As with Abraham and Ishmael, our prayers, like our perspectives, can often be short-sighted. They often do not take into account God's ability to break into history. How might we pray bolder prayers that seek God's glory rather than settling for what we see as 'possible' or 'attainable' from our own current life trajectories?

- In what ways are we being called to be champions of justice and righteousness? Have we helped others gain access to justice, spoken up for them when they couldn't or found a way to show mercy without simply abrogating the law?

- When have we been guilty of homosexual gang rape? Probably never. But have we invited those into our homes who have no family around? Have we protected those taking sanctuary under our roofs? Have we been generous in making what is ours available to others? It is in how we treat strangers – those who cannot pay us back – that we most reflect the love and way of God.

- Having God's promises fulfilled in our lives may require us to separate ourselves from those who impede it. This does not necessitate a judgement upon them, as they may not be leading us into sin, but simply away from what God has called us to. What ties do we have in our lives – even those we care very much about – that are a stumbling block or a diversion from following God wholeheartedly?

# 1 God of testing

**Genesis 22:1–19**

The *Akedah* or (near) sacrifice of Isaac is one of the most infamous passages in scripture. How could a good God command Abraham to kill his own son?

In verse 7, Isaac asks a penetrating question: 'Where is the lamb for the burnt offering?' Abraham's response is duplicitous and telling. Depending upon how it is punctuated, it can read either, 'God will see to the sacrifice, my son' or 'God will see for himself, the sacrifice – my son'. The first leads many translators to render the Hebrew *ra'ah*, 'to see', as 'provide'. However, the only times this ubiquitous verb is ever translated 'provide' are here in verses 8 and 14, and 1 Samuel 16:17 (better rendered 'look').

In fact, as the ram was not seen until after the angel stopped Abraham, declaring God's knowledge of his faith, 'provision' does not seem to be the point of the test (v. 1). God was not examining whether Abraham trusted his provision, but rather, God is watching his heart: will he give up his beloved son – his heir and the embodiment of all God's promises to him? Abraham's answer is essentially, 'God will see for himself that I am bringing the sacrifice, namely, my son.' The vagueness allows young Isaac to believe God is seeing to the lamb, while Abraham really answers God's test.

This test results in God knowing of Abraham's fear of him (v. 12). Did God not know this before? Terms like 'know' should be applied to God metaphorically, not because they don't indicate something real about him, but because divine descriptors shouldn't be reduced to their typical literal human limitations (e.g. I only know what I see). Here, it indicates that Abraham's fear of God, a common Old Testament expression of faith, was not made concrete until he raised the knife. Though nascent, until acted upon it was not real. God's 'knowing' simply indicates he experienced Abraham's faith first-hand as it was exercised. Thus, the mount of the Lord is not thereafter known as a place of provision (v. 14) – a mistaken belief held by those prior to the exile – but rather, a place where the hearts of those who claim him will be 'seen' – tested and refined.

# 2 The house of God

Genesis 28:10–22

Jacob flees his brother, but not without a blessing from his father. In fact, he is going to his uncle's, where he will find a wife of his own kin and faith, as opposed to his brother's pagan wives (28:8–9). Despite his flight, things are looking good for Jacob – so why the dream?

One of the distinct allusions of the ladder whose top reached heaven is that of the tower the men of Babel were trying to build (11:4). Here, we find the access point to the control room of the universe, which they mistakenly thought they'd achieved by their own joint efforts. In contrast, Jacob is utterly alone, on the move – not settling down, and does nothing whatsoever to find this access to heaven. God will not be found outside his will. Furthermore, though the Babelites were trying to make a name for themselves, Jacob will eventually have a name given to him from God. Finally, Jacob exclaims that this is the 'gate of heaven' (v. 17), which is actually what 'Babel' means. He had found by accident, or rather, by divine providence, what the Babelites thought they could create.

Jacob's stone pillow, as opposed to the bricks the Babelites tried to build with, becomes a standing stone or *matsebah*. These stones were used in the ancient Near East to indicate the presence of a holy place – most often due to the presence of a deity. This stone will now become not a testament to human ingenuity, but a record of God's presence not only here but also moving with Jacob.

God basically reissues the Abrahamic promises to Jacob, which at this point feels a bit unfair. Why eschew Abraham and Isaac's other offspring for this deceptive, low-life trickster? Part of the point is that it is God's grace – which he will show to whom he will (Exodus 33:19). But more than this, God gives him a more particular promise – that of his presence – 'until I have done what I have promised you' (v. 15). This promise is notably finite. It does not promise that Jacob will never be hurt, or that God will endorse everything Jacob does. It only ensures that God will be with Jacob, until he comes good on his promises. God's presence is not simply for the recipient's good, but for God's own purpose.

# 3 Sisterly struggles

**Genesis 29:16–35**

God 'sees' that Leah is 'unloved' by her husband (v. 31), a vision which prompts his intervention – he gives her children. This was perhaps an enticement for Jacob to pay her more attention than simply a consolation prize. Their names, however, track the condition of her faith. More telling is that she is the one who names these sons, as typically the father did this, evidence of Jacob's distancing himself from Leah and her children.

First, she has Reuben, which in Hebrew is similar to 'see, a son' (v. 32). It pictures a wife hoping her husband will be satisfied with finally becoming a father. Next in line is Simeon, whose name is related to the verb 'he hears' (v. 33), referring to Leah's forlorn cries for love. Levi comes from the verb 'to be attached' (v. 34), a state she hopes to achieve with her husband by virtue of having a son. By the time we get to Judah, Leah finally turns her attention from her intractable husband to God, saying, 'the Lord be praised' (v. 35). However, to say Leah is finally content with pleasing the Lord is premature, as her last son, Zebulun, still has her hoping, 'Now my husband will honour me' (30:20).

But God's grace to Leah becomes a trial for Rachel, whose womb he closes. Though loved by her husband (v. 20, 30), she becomes inflamed with jealousy. She resorts to a tactic used by her grandmother-in-law, Sarah, surrendering her maid to her husband to have a surrogate child. Leah follows suit. Only when Leah is done bearing children is Rachel given a child. Though this ought to give her satisfaction, the name says otherwise – 'Joseph': 'may he add' (30:23).

Ironically, we have one sister who ends up with loads of children, but only desires to be loved. The sister who is loved only seems to care for the children she cannot have.

Only when Rachel is on her deathbed does Jacob finally intervene. Instead of allowing her to name his final son 'son of my sorrow', a name that would haunt him all his life, he changes the name to 'son of my right hand' (35:18), which speaks to Jacob's own strength and the son who becomes his most treasured child.

# 4 God's white flag

**Genesis 32:3–32**

Can a man defeat God? Jacob was no weakling, as he moved a massive stone away from a well by himself so that Rachel could water her sheep (29:10). But who could actually defeat their maker, and why try?

Jacob is already headed to reconcile with his estranged brother Esau, though he has heard a company of 400 men is coming his way. Hence, he splits his family into two, so that Esau might not kill all of them, and he himself hangs back at the river (vv. 7–8). To understand what is going on, we must remember how Jacob got here. First, he traded a pot of stew for his brother's birthright when he returned famished from hunting. Then, he disguised himself and stole his brother's firstborn blessing from his blind father on his deathbed. This puts Esau on the warpath, and Jacob in flight to his uncle. There, he gets a taste of his own medicine when his uncle switches his bride for her sister. However, he continues to play the swindler in taking the best of his uncle's flocks. Now, he is returning to the land God had promised him. Though he will need to make things right with Esau in order to go there, this is actually secondary. He first needs to do business with God.

This is why it is so significant that, though he cannot overpower God, Jacob will not give up. His determination to pursue God's blessing, God's way, is a huge volte-face. Jacob no longer seeks success in his own underhanded power, but wrestles with God himself to attain his blessing. This turn of events is required for God to rename him. Without the contest, God could not have given him the name Israel, 'the one who strives with God and prevails'. It is not necessarily that he prevails over God. In ancient Near Eastern wrestling, there were ways of defeating one's opponent without actually subduing him. Each wrestler would wear a cloth sash around his waist, and the wrestler who was able to take the other's belt off won.

Here, Jacob neither overpowers nor defeats God. He prevails not over God, but *upon him*, and *because of* him. We now find a man, though still wisely taking precautions, leading his family (33:3), humbly addressing his brother and giving rather than taking.

# 5 Rape of Dinah

**Genesis 34**

The story of Dinah's rape is as pointed as it is tragic. There are some clues that this story merely uses Dinah as a foil to uncover the blackened hearts of both her brothers and the men of the land. Not that her fate didn't matter to the writer, but the initial shock of her abuse served to make the men's reactions in the story even more appalling.

Though Shechem's love for Dinah is mentioned repeatedly, it is the financial gain to which he and his father appeal, both to get her brothers and father on board, as well as to get their own kinsman to become circumcised and 'one people' (v. 16) with Dinah's family. All they see is a bullish market.

Jacob for his part, after he hears of her rape, does nothing, because his 'sons were with his livestock in the field' (v. 5). However, even after they come in, he remains silent. In fact, Jacob never responds to the rape itself.

It is his second and third sons who do. In contrast with their passive father, Simeon and Levi act deceitfully and kill a whole village to avenge their sister. We find out after the fact that Jacob finds this disgraceful, removing them from his good graces. This causes his favour to fall on his fourth son, Judah, from whom, as Israel later prophesies, the Messiah will come (49:8–10). (His firstborn, Reuben, had disqualified himself by sleeping with one of his father's concubines.)

Though Jacob rebukes his sons for their genocidal rage, this is mainly for making him odious to the people of the land. The brothers poignantly retort, 'Should he treat our sister as a harlot?' (v. 31). They refer to Dinah as 'our sister', rather than 'your daughter', just as verse 1 had emphasised her as Leah's daughter. The impact of Jacob's favouritism against Leah and her children is snowballing out of control.

The phrase 'a disgraceful thing in Israel' has an anachronistic ring (v. 7). The immediate referent is Shechem's rape, but it comes across as a later interpolation, as currently the tribes are not a nation and are living in other people's lands. Could the editor be posing a larger question to a now landed Israelite audience? In each of these cases, the men seem far more interested in their trading prospects, safety or acquisition of wealth than the honour of this young woman.

# 6 Vows fulfilled

After the debacle at Shechem, Jacob heads south along the hill country to where God first promised to be with him and he vowed that God would be his god – at Bethel. It is mentioned twice that God appeared to Jacob when he fled from his brother (vv. 1, 7). This recalls a time in Jacob's life not only when he was in dire need, but when he was also swamped with guilt. He was a swindler who had done nothing worthy of God's attention, nor even worshipped him prior to this point, and yet God appeared to *him*. *Then*. While still up to his old tricks with his uncle, God spoke to him again, prompting a reconciliation with his brother. Now, God commands Jacob to go to Bethel, to fulfil his vows. Like the first time he went to Bethel, God protects Jacob – this time sending dread of him upon the surrounding peoples (v. 5; compare 28:15). Jacob not only completes his vows but presents himself before God a changed man.

In worshipping God, Jacob first purifies his family. They have been defiled not only by Shechem's rape, but by the blood on their own hands from the slaughter. The putting away of the idols is not only a commitment to Yahweh as their (only) God, reminiscent of Jacob's promise in 28:21, but perhaps also a fulfilment of his commitment to tithe (28:22). The idols may have been spoils from the Shechemites, rather than tokens of personal syncretistic practices, but in any case, they are removed without hesitation.

However, Jacob's transformation is not a harbinger of easy times ahead. Not only does his mother's nurse die – the only reminder of the one who sent him on this journey in the first place – but his firstborn sleeps with his concubine Bilhah. This is likely more than lust-induced behaviour, but a calculated move to keep the favoured wife's maid from becoming the 'new' favoured wife over his own mother, Leah. Finally, his beloved Rachel also dies in childbirth on the way to Bethlehem.

Despite these tragedies and underlying troubles, some things end well, as Jacob finally reunites with his father at Hebron, and he and Esau show some solidarity in honouring their father at his death.

# Guidelines

- Where have we sought God's provision instead of seeking him? Abraham's test illuminated how he valued things in comparison with their source – even his family, his heir and the fulfilment of God's own promises. None should compare to God himself. Do we honestly seek God just for God himself?

- In what ways have we presumed God's endorsement of our lives? Where have we expanded his promise to license all of our desires and behaviours, rather than the ones which he has communicated and which bring him glory?

- The grass is always greener. We always want what we don't have and take too little stock in what we do. But worse, we often place our happiness in someone else's hands or in the outcome of events over which we have no control. Can we seek God for contentment – not settling for apathy?

- Like Jacob, we desire to be self-made men and women. We want to overcome adversity by our own cleverness, stubbornness and skill. But how far will we go to achieve success? Will we turn our determination to God and seek, even demand, his blessing?

- What sin do we allow to go unaddressed? Jacob not only allowed his daughter's rape to slip silently by, but also harboured a favouritism among his children which prompted them to sin and wrought terrible consequences. What personal foibles or preferences do we have that might actually be sin, causing larger ripple effects in our family and sphere of influence?

- God can and does speak to us at the oddest times. We neither induce him to speak through our worship, nor prevent his speaking through our sin. He speaks to whom and when he wills. That said, it is important to fulfil our vows to him. Jacob's vows helped establish the worship of Yahweh within his own family, both dedicating important spiritual milestones in their family history, and also actively trusting God to deliver them on their way to their dedication. Have we given up on God's speaking to us? Have we given him what we promised, and taken time to demonstrate to our family the role God has played in our lives?

## FURTHER READING

David Clines, 'The Image of God in Man', *Tyndale Bulletin 19* (1968), pp. 53–103.

David Clines, *The Theme of the Pentateuch* (Bloomsbury Publishing, 1997).

Victor P. Hamilton, *The Book of Genesis 1–17 (The New International Commentary on the Old Testament)* (William B. Eerdmans, 1990).

Brian C. Howell, *In the Eyes of God: A metaphorical approach to biblical anthropomorphic language* (Pickwick, 2013).

Kenneth A. Mathews, *Genesis 1–11:26 (The New American Commentary)* (Broadman & Holman, 1996).

Gordon J. Wenham, *Genesis 1–15 (Word Biblical Commentary)* (Word Books, 1987).

Gordon J. Wenham, *Genesis 16–50 (Word Biblical Commentary)* (Word Books, 1994).

# The pathways of God

## John Rackley

For over 30 years, I have visited the Bible lands leading pilgrimages. Some of the most moving and memorable experiences of my time there were walking ancient paths and tracks, many of which predated anything else I saw.

Sometimes we were climbing on paths laid down centuries ago for reasons of trade, war or faith. At others, we were knee-deep in soft sand with no sign of a path. We relied upon the reassuring confidence of our guide to get us where we were heading. He was the way!

Occasionally, we were walking in places mentioned in the Bible but often we were following a route that predated all written scripture.

Scripture could be given the subtitle: 'the pathways of God'. They are pathways which lead through the human experience of God's people. The pathways of God is a metaphor for the movement of God in the lives of people and the greater world. He makes a new way but also follows the old ways.

He is always the companion. Some encounters with God are rightly seen as unique to a particular person or location. Yet are they not also examples of just the sort of thing that God does with people?

The path we tread with God is always a path into the heart of our need and faith. As the Lord commanded his people at a time of bewilderment and insecurity, 'Stand at the crossroads and look, and ask for the ancient paths, where the good way lies; and walk in it, and find rest for your souls' (Jeremiah 6:16).

In this series, I will be examining some of these pathways as they arose in the life of Jesus. I am asking us to consider how they might heighten our own appreciation of the work of God in our lives.

Quotations are from the New Revised Standard Version.

# 1 The pathway of our ancestors

**Luke 2:1–7; 21–33**

I am held in my mother's arms in the centre of the photograph. Around us are my father, grandparents and godparents. I am draped in a christening gown which has been used for generations by my family for such occasions in the little parish church which stands rock-sure in the background.

It is a snapshot of a moment in my life. Here was my family. They were the link to my ancestors, who were workers for the local landowner and fishermen, members of the Church of England, Tory and Liberals. But something new was going to happen. My father decided I should be brought up in the Baptist way. It took many years before I rediscovered my Anglican DNA!

We all have a heritage. It is the environment and spiritual hinterland from which we emerge. It is a pathway that we cannot choose. It is given us and, early in life, occasions such as christenings mark out our journey into the future. But do they?

Jeremiah wisely advises his troubled people, lost, without a sense of purpose, to seek the ancient paths (Jeremiah 6:16). In them, they would gain perspective and a sense of belonging to something greater than their small moment in time. But it was the same prophet who spoke later of a new relationship with God, never known before (Jeremiah 31:31–32). The ancestral pathway was a preparation for something new.

The baby Jesus was placed firmly within the demands of Roman law (vv. 1–4) and Jewish custom (vv. 21–24).

But something new was going to happen.

We cannot blame Mary and Joseph any more than my family. They were doing what was expected and sanctioned by the powers temporal and spiritual. But the ancient paths are about an eternal way, as some translations render Jeremiah, and also the healthcare for both Jesus and Mary that required priestly sanction. Furthermore, circumcision was the great defining sign of God's blessing of his people and his paternal care of their path. But this does not limit the freedom of God.

As Simeon pointed out (vv. 29–32), the child given a name of special grace by a divine source had a destiny that would change his family forever and question the spiritual destiny of his people. This child would grow to question the tradition and challenge the status quo and, through his obedience, enable the purpose of God for us all to be initiated (Galatians 4:4–6). Great is his faithfulness!

# 2 The pathway to choice

Luke 2:39–52

One early spring, Jesus went missing. He had turned back from the path to his home town because he found the home of God. His parents had naturally looked among friends and family, but Jesus had been drawn away from them.

Was this the start of his search for anyone who responded seriously to God? Later in life, he would call such people his true family (Luke 8:19–21).

Choice is highly valued in our society, especially in our education system. From early years, parents and children are made to face choices that will affect their future pathway. In a more questionable way, I have regularly been told by parents who wish the church to do something for their newborn that, of course, in our day and age, they will not be expecting the child to come to church later on 'because we want him to make up his own mind'.

A laudable aspiration, which recognises that choices around faith and God are significantly personal, is undermined by a seeming desire to avoid the process. It sounds so tolerant, but I wonder.

Jesus did choose and, against his parents' expectations, he took seriously what he had seen and heard at Passover. It is often suggested that this was the time of Jesus's bar mitzvah, but he was too young at twelve and this custom had not been established at that time. Yet it was expected that at that age a boy would be receiving deeper teaching by a rabbi. So, in the temple, Jesus was doing his research! He was taking his faith seriously. Who would be his teacher?

A Methodist lay preacher explained to me that, after attending a series of Holy Week services, he came to a moment of choice. Was he going to walk the path of Christ or not? There were no two ways about it.

Turning to Christ may be assisted by a moment of inspiration or epiphany, but more deeply it is a matter of choice which affects our total humanity immersed in divine love (Luke 10:25–27).

It is a choice that is most active when we are most under stress. Gordon Wilson lost his daughter Marie in the Enniskillen bombing in 1987. He declared that he forgave the bombers. In a matter-of-fact way, he stated that his church had taught him about forgiveness – so he had no other choice.

An informed choice at one point in his life directed his path into the future – whatever may arise.

# 3 The pathway to disclosure

**Luke 4:1–10**

Where might a person full of the Holy Spirit end up? The wilderness might not be our first choice, but that is what happens to Jesus. As he made his way through a hard landscape, the tempter disclosed his hand and Jesus spoilt his tactics. Satan was trying to prevent Jesus starting the journey begun at his baptism, knowing that he would face defeat if he could not get Jesus off this path (John 12:31). Jesus would have none of it. In resisting the temptations, Jesus disclosed his calling from his Father God.

If we are to identify with any of the experiences of Jesus, we need to hold two things in tension. Like Jesus himself, we will be exposed to the reality of our vulnerability and human fragility resulting in temptation and distorting visions of reality. Yet, also like Jesus, we are enfolded in the truth that we have been given a path to follow. It too arises from our baptism, where we accept the dynamic of dying to self and rising into the glory of God's will for us.

We can discern the depths of our lives and vocation only if we surrender our self-centred view of reality. This is hard to do. It is unsettling to relinquish who we think we are, and scary to stop clinging to what we have and what we do.

Yet it is only when we inwardly surrender our smaller, culturally formed identities that we can be open to the Spirit, who waits for us and longs to disclose our true nature as children of the will and kingdom of God.

The Judean wilderness overlooks Jericho and faces Mount Nebo across the Jordan Valley. Jesus stood within the promised land which Moses could not enter. The long years of Israel's faith and failure, which were equally challenged and embraced by the righteous mercy of God, separated Jesus and Moses. Yet the Son of God inherited the prophetic teaching of Israel's leader (Deuteronomy 34:10) and enriched it with the Spirit.

Such high places as Moses and Jesus inhabited set us apart from ourselves, our routines, and give us a different perspective. What can emerge from such times may be a change of direction or a repentance which will take us on to a path of disclosure that deepens our resolve, resists the devil and gives glory to God.

# 4 The pathway to awareness

**Luke 9:28–36**

Luke deliberately tells us that Jesus is on a path which will lead to the cross and beyond. He describes this as an exodus (v. 31), reminding us of the great foundation story of the Torah. All believers are in an exodus; it is a journey into a greater awareness of God and us.

Peter, James and John, without realising it, are now on that path with Jesus.

Fishermen don't climb mountains. It was beyond their experience. The unfamiliarity of what Jesus was asking them to do was the necessary first step into a new awareness. It is the unsettling experience of not knowing what is going on; but in this struggle of Peter and the others, we have a foundation parable for our own journey of faith.

Peter and his friends were given a new awareness, a new way of seeing Jesus. Peter tries to relate the experience of the cloud and the voice to what his faith had taught him from the Jewish scriptures (Deuteronomy 16:13–17).

Then God interrupts: 'This is my Son, my Chosen; listen to him!'

All their previous spiritual and religious experience now had to be considered through a Christ-shaped filter.

Although the trek up the mountain began in unfamiliarity, it became a route into fresh insight. Jesus was more than he appeared.

The inclusion of Moses and Elijah has been described as a kind of salvation-history summit conference. They have much in common with the disciples. Both had received a deeper awareness of the presence of God on a mountainside. They, like the disciples of Jesus, saw what was hidden. Their struggles and their faith were brought to a place where the wider picture could be seen.

Moses saw the destiny of his people. He was a contributor to the path God had chosen for them. Elijah received the insight and courage to take on what was in store for him.

They were given the experience, but they were not the vision. So it is with the followers of Jesus. He is our destiny. We are called to walk with him into greater belief and deeper faith.

We must never mistake our ideas, projects or churches for the vision God pursues for us. We have limited insight. We are to follow the one who is both the pioneer of our faith and brings it to total fulfilment. We will not be able to escape the cross on the way to the conclusion of that exodus (Hebrews 12:1–2).

# 5  The pathway to the edge of experience

**Luke 17:11–19**

Jesus was travelling though border territory on his way to Jerusalem. He arrived at the outskirts of a village: a place on the edge of two regions. He and his disciples were on unfamiliar ground. Galilee had been left behind. Jesus had done this before. It seems to have been a pattern (see Mark 5:1; 8:27; Matthew 15:21).

It seems to have been the policy of Jesus. He went with his disciples into experiences that were new, different and challenging. He then expected them to watch him.

The healing occurred. Some were made better; only one was made whole. Notice how this happens. One man returned. We are told what he did but only then who he was (v. 16). Praise! Worship! Thanksgiving! Identity! A Samaritan, a renegade Jew.

This explains why he could not go with the others. The illness which had tied them together was gone. Their priest would not bless him. He had nowhere to go. So he came to Jesus. The leprosy which gave him an identity that he could share with the others had been stripped away. But could Jews and a Samaritan have anything to do with each other from then on?

Yes, if the Jew were Jesus. With his true identity uncovered, the nameless Samaritan and Jesus reached out to each other. They created a prophetic relationship based on the recognition of who Jesus is, a relationship that challenged the conventions and traditions of both Jewish and Samaritan worlds.

For the disciples, this was an important time of teaching as they watched, probably keeping their distance. The twelve had nothing to say.

Perhaps they were troubled that someone so unlike them was acting so like a disciple of Jesus.

So why did Jesus do this? What happens when we go to the edge of experience?

It gives us a glimpse of something different and invites us into a journey of discovery.

Walking on the borders allows us to see where we have come from and where we might go.

Going to the edge enables us to become a connection across the borders that divide, and assist both sides of the divide to relate to each other.

Jesus took his disciples to the borders. He invited them to meet the people on their margins – to listen to their needs – and invited them to establish common ground for all to stand on. He is showing them what it means to be people living in the kingdom of God.

# 6 The pathway to restoration

Luke 19:1–10

This is a story of two journeys. The first is the journey of Jesus, who had turned his face in the direction of Jerusalem (Luke 9:51). His encounter with Zacchaeus actually starts as Jesus arrives outside the entrance to the city, where he is met by a beggar (Luke 18:35—19:2).

Jesus heals the man, but the crowd, made up of locals and fellow pilgrims like Jesus going up to the great festival of the Passover, are proving difficult to handle. Kenneth Bailey suggests there would have been city dignitaries ready to offer hospitality to the travellers and, in particular, the notorious rabbi, Jesus of Nazareth. But Jesus wasn't to be stopped (v. 1). He was not prepared to accept the city's hospitality (See further reading.)

As Jesus enters the city, Zacchaeus starts his journey and seeks a place to see Jesus. It is likely that the sycamore trees would have been farmed outside the city. They were large trees and the city was small.

Zacchaeus is not running away. He doesn't want to be involved with an excitable crowd. So the senior tax officer, loathed by the city, unwelcome at synagogue but longing to see Jesus, forgets his dignity and runs to find a place where he can observe, unseen. At this point, the two journeys meet.

Jesus invites himself to the house of Zacchaeus. In doing so, Jesus, who has turned down the welcome of the city, deflects the attitude of the crowd from Zacchaeus on to himself; it makes all the difference to Zacchaeus.

As Zacchaeus responds to this invitation and explains what he is going to do about it, Jesus adds his own interpretation: 'Today salvation has come to this house' (v. 9) – and it is going to stay. The tax collector is always going to live where the liberating, forgiving power of God is at home. Jesus goes on: 'Because he too is a son of Abraham.'

Zacchaeus had always been a child of God, a member of God's people; he and others had lost sight of that crucial identity. For the mission of Jesus was 'to seek out and to save the lost' (v. 10).

The people are left with a memory of a rabbi, a healer who took the shame of Zacchaeus on himself; a salvation which he would share with the world a few days later from the cross.

## Guidelines

- Recall any pathways you have found or travelled along. Why do you remember them now? What significance do they have for you? Are any of them a metaphor for your own journey of faith?

- If you have a picture of a family gathering, such as a christening, spend some time looking at its content: the faces, clothing, setting, time of year, how it was at that time in your home town or nation. What might it say about your ancestral path? What was your family hoping for? What has happened since? Are you still on their pathway?

- Jesus chose to stay behind in the temple. Is there a similar moment in your life which has shaped your trust in God ever since?

- Do you need to confess that there are mountaintop experiences which you have resisted and so failed to see Jesus in a new light? Are you ready to pray for the faith required for another climb in order to receive the grace of God in a life-enriching way?

- Are there borderlands which you are approaching with God? Do you feel prepared or are you hesitant? What might you learn from the man who returned to Jesus?

The first collective name given to followers of Jesus after Pentecost was 'the Way' (Acts 9:2). It demonstrates their attitude to faith: they were a movement. This is faithful living going beyond the patterns of inherited religion and invites this prayer:

Lord of many pathways,
May we have no fear when our paths become unfamiliar
and old convictions seem to offer no help.
Let your presence hidden in the everyday material of our life
speak through the people and events we share.
May we respond with trust
and walk with you along new pathways of hope into your eternity.
Amen

**FURTHER READING**

Kenneth E. Bailey, *Jesus through Middle Eastern Eyes* (SPCK, 2008).
Joel B. Green, *The Gospel of Luke (New International Commentary)* (Eerdmans, 1997).
Robert Macfarlane, *The Old Ways* (Penguin, 2012).
Andrew D. Mayes, *Beyond the Edge* (SPCK, 2013).

# Isaiah 1—39

## Torsten Uhlig

The book of Isaiah has been called by some the 'fifth gospel'. Its reception as a collection of words of encouragement, comfort and predictions to Jesus of Nazareth has been amplified by Handel's phenomenal 'Messiah' and the prominent appearance of individual verses on Christian postcards and posters, and in hymns and social media postings. However, a closer look at the book as a whole, and at Isaiah 1—39 in particular, shows how diverse the sayings in this prophetic book are, how its contrasting images of God challenge and how turbulent the occurrences of the promised saviour figure appear. But it is precisely in persevering in the confrontation of these challenges that we may become aware of the depth of the words of this breathtaking book and its transforming power.

The prophet Isaiah lived in the eighth century BC in Judah. It was a time of economic prosperity on the one hand and of increasing political turbulences on the other. The economic growth benefited only a few at the expense of the poor, contradicting some of the fundamental principles among the people of the Lord. At the same time, Assyria expanded from the river Tigris, dominating most of the ancient Near East down to the borders of Egypt, which left both kingdoms of Israel and Judah trapped within the pincer movement of Assyria from the north and Egypt from the south.

Isaiah 1—39 presents the prophet Isaiah addressing the situation within Judah and Jerusalem and correlating it to the rise of Assyria, and puts it in a broader universal context that exceeds the immediate time of Isaiah. Confronted with the specific issues of the eighth century in Judah and Jerusalem, readers of Isaiah 1—39 encounter diverse images of God and complex foundations for hope that even encompass judgement and visions of justice.

I have included many biblical references for those who wish to explore my comments in greater detail. Quotations are taken from the New Revised Standard Version.

# 1 God's rebellious children (the theme of 'God's people')

**Isaiah 1:2–20**

These verses at the very beginning of Isaiah address the people of God as his children. From the outset, they are characterised as rebellious children (v. 2). Yet, like no other book in the Hebrew Bible, Isaiah associates the fate of God's people with other nations and the universe. It is thus not a mere rhetorical means when the addressees hear about themselves via the address to the heavens and earth (v. 2). The history of God's people takes place within and presupposes creation as much as the relationship between God and his people affects creation.

Verses 2–9 start with an honest evaluation of the current relationship between God and his people in Isaiah's time. It provides some harsh critique, alludes to some consequences and states some fundamental principles for any future relationship. Given God's care for his children, it is inconceivable that they lack any understanding (vv. 2–3). None of God's educational measures changed their course of going astray (vv. 4–6). This has led to the situation in 701BC, when the foreign Assyrian empire devastated much of the land of Judah and besieged Jerusalem, which only survived due to God's rescue (see Isaiah 36—37). It has been left like a booth, which served as a lookout or a shelter for a family, where they could sleep during harvest (v. 8).

From a temporal perspective, these remarks point towards the end of Isaiah's ministry under the reign of Hezekiah. But from a spatial perspective, these verses depict a movement from the outer limits of life (heaven and earth) via the land of Judah and her cities to the capital Jerusalem. The next section (vv. 10–20) leads right into Jerusalem and even further to the temple. This spatial movement of centralisation coincides with the temporal rewinding, as verses 10–20 presuppose an earlier, more comfortable situation. Here, God rejects the people's services and prayers because they are contradicted by their current behaviour (v. 15). The passage leads to what God expects of his people (vv. 16–17) and connects the people's future life with their future behaviour (vv. 19–20) on the basis of the paradoxical statement or question about sins being washed white again (v. 18). This strategy of internalisation – from the outer limits of life to the inner centre of the addressee's will ('If you are *willing*…', v. 19) indicates that the will of the addressees is a central issue and their obedience far from taken for granted.

## 2 God's (un-)faithful bride (the theme of 'Zion as the city of God')

**Isaiah 1:21–31; 2:1–4**

Ever since David transferred the ark of the covenant to Jerusalem (2 Samuel 6; Psalm 132:8, 13), it was regarded as God's chosen dwelling place, where his salvific presence could be experienced. Originally just one hill in Jerusalem, Zion was soon synonymous with the people of the city of Jerusalem. But sometimes, when Zion is mentioned, it does not simply refer to the inhabitants of Jerusalem but stands for the city itself. The behaviour of her inhabitants affects Jerusalem, but they are not identical.

As in other cultures of the ancient Near East, life in Judah and Jerusalem is based on the interconnection of all actions. In this context, justice is understood as 'acting for each other'. The connection of deed and consequence, an important theme in the wisdom literature, is related to this concept of justice and righteousness.

Jerusalem, whose name alludes to shalom/peace by 'salem', symbolises justice and righteousness (1:21). But the prophet has to lament that this original character has fundamentally changed. Now, Jerusalem is to be called a 'whore', who is unfaithful. Consequently, Jerusalem will experience judgement, so that she is refined, as silver is purified by melting away all dross.

Isaiah 2:1–4 presents a contrasting Jerusalem to 1:21–31. Despite using different metaphors, they also complement one another. Hence, these verses do not simply depict Jerusalem 'before and after'. Isaiah 2:1–4 goes beyond the former character of Jerusalem. It introduces a new perspective on Jerusalem, which heightens the problems in Isaiah's days all the more: Jerusalem is there not only for herself but has a universal calling. Jerusalem is to be exalted, and as such she is to become the centre of the world (2:2–3). Jerusalem is to become the source for a worldwide process of transformation that is rooted in God's just jurisdiction (2:4) and his teaching for living in justice and righteousness (2:3). The result of this change in Jerusalem will be universal recasting of arms into tools for agriculture (2:4).

# 3  God's beloved vineyard (the theme of 'justice')

Justice is an important theme in the book of Isaiah. Various passages address the issue of what God expects of his people and how they relate to this. But what does justice mean? How does God react when his people do not live according to justice and righteousness? These are some of the concerns that are illustrated by Isaiah 5:1–7.

This passage starts like a touching love song that someone sings on behalf of his best friend. As cultivating a vineyard might have been a common metaphor for courting someone (compare Song of Songs 7:8–9, 12; 8:11–12), the song seems to reflect the devotion and despair in a romantic relationship. But all of a sudden, the vineyard is identified with the addressees and the vintner turns out to be the Lord (v. 7). Accordingly, justice is not simply a standard according to which someone has to live; justice means to pass on the good that the Lord has already provided.

First, there is the love, care and blessing of God, like a vintner who cares for his vineyard. The consequence of this love of God should be people sharing God's blessings with each other, in particular with the poor, and returning it to the Lord in praise, like a vineyard yielding good fruits. This is what righteousness in Israel and the ancient Near East is all about: maintaining the circle of blessing. But it does also belong to this concept of righteousness that those who disturb this connection are judged. Isaiah 5:1–7 claims that it is not just a few who have disturbed the circle of righteous behaviour, but that the whole people must be characterised as those who pervert God's blessings. Hence, in order to keep righteousness, God has to judge the people.

After Isaiah 5:1–7, particular examples illustrate the devastating situation in Judah and Jerusalem. Contrary to divine laws and fundamental principles of justice in Judah, some dispossess the poor, destroying the foundation of their living (v. 8). Drunkards disturb the principle of 'acting for each other' as well as those who are lazy (v. 22). Jurisdiction is misled (v. 23) and the rules of communication that are fundamental presuppositions for a just society are bent (5:18–20). The people misuse God's blessings. So, he intervenes by his wrath, his devotion for justice, as only by this means can a just order in society be re-established.

# 4 God's disturbing presence
## (the theme of 'God as king')

When the people of Jerusalem came to the temple in order to 'seek the face' of God (see Psalm 27), they were looking for blessings, God's help in individual trials (righteousness) and his protection from other enemies. Their confidence in the Lord was dependent on his kingship over all the earth (6:3; Psalm 93). His throne was 'high and lofty' (v. 1) and his glory filled all the earth (v. 3; corresponding to the seams of his robe, which filled the temple, v. 1).

But when Isaiah saw the Lord, his presence changed from an assurance of blessing and well-being to a threat of judgement. Seraphim (fiery ones), dangerous serpents with wings (14:29; 30:6; Numbers 21:6), accompany God. The 'pivots on the thresholds' (v. 4) shake and the temple fills with smoke (v. 4) so that the 'face of God' cannot be seen anymore. This vision of judgement leads Isaiah to fear for his life (v. 5), because only those with clean hands, pure hearts and truthful communication will receive blessing and righteousness of God at the temple (Psalm 24). But Isaiah is a man of 'unclean lips' and lives among people of 'unclean lips' (v. 5), which is specified already in 3:8–9 and 5:18–20.

Yet, he does not die. His lips are purified, not by forgiveness but by the judgement of burning his lips (vv. 6–7). Now he lives beyond judgement, but he volunteers to speak to 'this people' who still live before judgement. While this judgement is explained and announced in general already in Isaiah 5, Isaiah 6 focuses on the specific judgement of their communication, which is carried out through the 'hardening' message of Isaiah (vv. 9–10).

For Isaiah's audience, his report poses the questions: how will they respond to his message, what is the state of their heart and how can they relate to God? In fact, it takes quite some time reading through the book of Isaiah until the ministry of an individual servant, whose commission for Israel and the nations is reported in Isaiah 49:1–12, renews the communicative abilities (50:4–5) and recreates the heart of the book's audience (51:7; 53:1–10).

# 5 God's ambiguous presence (the theme of 'judgement and salvation')

Isaiah 7:1–19; 8:1–10

This passage is about the effects of Isaiah's ministry upon his audience – the king of Jerusalem and the people of Judah and Jerusalem. At the time of Isaiah, the northern kingdom Israel and its neighbour Syria (Aram) had already become 'vassal states' of Assyria. But they wanted to form a coalition against Assyria in about 735BC in order to liberate themselves. When Judah, who was still independent, refused to enter into this coalition, Israel and Syria attacked Judah in order to install another king who was supportive of their policy (7:1).

In this situation, the prophet Isaiah addresses King Ahaz (Isaiah 7) and the people as a whole (Isaiah 8). In both cases, his sons serve as signs by their names that communicate an ambiguous message (7:3; 8:1–4). 'Shear-jashub' ('a remnant will return', 7:3) and 'Maher-shalal-hash-baz' ('the spoil speeds, the prey hastens', 8:1, 3) could be understood as announcements of a quick defeat of the attacking nations Israel and Aram (a remnant of them will return defeated and they quickly become spoil and prey themselves). The question is how the king and the people will react to this word of assurance. When they 'stand firm in faith' (7:9) and put their faith in 'the waters of Shiloah' (8:6, a phrase referring to God's care and protection for Jerusalem similar to Psalm 46:4), these names indicate salvation. But if they don't, these names indicate their future, too.

Either way, God is present. But as the king and the people reject Isaiah's message, God is present ambiguously. The king, instead of trusting in God, chooses to call Assyria for help, which is reported in 2 Kings 16:7–9 and seems to be presupposed in Isaiah 7. The people, contrastingly, welcome Israel and Aram (8:6). In response to these reactions, Isaiah announces the birth of another child, Immanuel (7:14). It may indicate a rejection of the actual king by God, as it implies installing another king. Instead, God is present with Jerusalem and his people by Immanuel, which means 'God is with us'. Hence, he rescues them from Israel and Aram, 'these two smouldering stumps of firebrands' (7:4). But what God initiates in the life of this child will develop only through the immediate judgement, as God will tighten the 'tongs' of Egypt and Assyria and the one whom King Ahaz invited will come not to rescue but to devastate (8:7–8).

# 6 God's new king (the theme of 'the Messiah')

The contrasts could hardly be starker. On the one hand, there is darkness, gloom and anguish (9:1–2), Assyrian military boots (9:5), a heavy yoke on the shoulder (9:4); on the other hand, there is light (9:2), joy (9:3), a newborn child and a righteous government on his shoulder (9:6).

While the exact historical reference of Isaiah 9:1–6 is difficult to determine, it is reasonable to relate it to Assyrian invasions in Israel in the eighth century BC. The gloom of these days is not neglected. Further chapters even show that the God of Israel is behind all of that (10:5–19). But here, the audience of the book of Isaiah learns about the new government of the Lord, accomplished by a new king in a new era. While the heavy burden and brutal military force of Assyria can be felt in many verses, the contrasting way of God's government appears: by a child, God overcomes the oppressor; in the government of this child, God's providence will be experienced, which is expressed in the names of the child (9:6). As the child Immanuel stands for God's presence in judgement and salvation (7:14; 8:7–10), the newborn child incorporates God's counsel that is miraculous, the power of God, his loving relationship to Israel and Judah that recalls a father (see also 1:2–3) and his will to act as prince of peace.

Some speak of a 'messianic triptych' in Isaiah 7, 9 and 11. Indeed, there is a movement from the announcement of the birth of a new king (7:14) to the celebration of his birth (9:1–6) to his inauguration (11:1–6). But we are not to miss the threatening implications. As much as these passages announce a new king, they mean at the same time that the present king in Judah is rejected.

While Isaiah 9 concentrates on the turn of an era and its effects on Judah and Jerusalem, Isaiah 11 highlights the universal impact of the inauguration of this new king and the source of his just government. As the new king is equipped with God's Spirit, his rule will result in knowledge, righteousness and peace on the whole earth. The Spirit of God is a dynamic force that changes and furthers perception and understanding.

# Guidelines

These passages challenge our way of thinking about God as much as they challenge the readers of the book of Isaiah about themselves. God's care for justice and righteousness is mediated through a love song (5:1–7). God who relates himself to his people like a father to his children rejects prayers (1:15). God who is universal king hides himself from his people in order to judge them (6:4–11). The announcement of his new king is inseparably linked with judgement and salvation at one and the same time. God rejects the present king but remains faithful to his promises so that he humiliates himself in retaining kings in Jerusalem (Isaiah 7, 9 and 11).

The readers are challenged not only to act according to God's blessings, but also to will God's will with all their heart (1:19). The whole book of Isaiah indicates that this formation of the human heart is achieved only by the detour of hardening them (6:9–10). But this focus on the internal condition of Isaiah's audience corresponds to the charismatic equipment of the new king (Isaiah 11). Thereby, Isaiah's message confronts us with a God who loves and hates, cares and abandons, rejects prayers and continues to speak for the sake of the refinement of Zion (1:21–31) and the internal transformation of her inhabitants, so that all nations want to learn justice and righteousness from the God who dwells there (2:1–4). It is not easy reading these passages, but it might lead to allowing God to work within us.

# 1 Hope of universal judgement (the theme of 'the day of the Lord')

**Isaiah 13:1–12, 17–22**

There is no doubt that many aspects of this passage are disturbing for today's readers. But imagine a time when there was no escape from the superiority of an expanding superpower, when there were no rules of military engagement, no restrictions for humanitarian reasons. Against Babylon, the all-present superpower of the sixth century BC, the present passage announces a day of the Lord, by which God not only sets limits to every superpower but actually judges them. More specifically, Isaiah 13 announces that Babylon will suffer what she has inflicted upon other nations in the first place (compare 13:16, 18 with the experiences of inhabitants of Jerusalem, when Babylon destroyed the capital of Judah in Lamentations 2:21; 5:11). As in other parts of the Old Testament and the book of Isaiah, God works together with human resources and powers to exercise his rule: according to 10:5–19, the Lord uses Assyria as his 'rod' to judge Israel and Judah; 13:17 announces the 'stirring up' of the Medes, a rising empire east of Mesopotamia, against Babylon.

However, Babylon here seems to be more than the empire of the sixth century. It incorporates and typifies a tyrannical power that wants to replace God, as the next passage makes clear (Isaiah 14). It is the symbolic representative of any evil power, which incorporates in itself different kingdoms, like Assyria (14:24–27), the historical Babylon (Isaiah 21), Tyre (Isaiah 23) and Edom (Isaiah 34).

The Lord establishes his universal kingship even against this kind of superpower, and if necessary by the means of judging such tyrants. This passage shows that judgement is not necessarily threatening or negative. For those who are oppressed, God's judgement of the oppressors means salvation. It is this perspective that is revealed by Isaiah 13 and which forms the foil for all subsequent oracles that are delivered in respect to particular nations, superpowers and vassal states alike. But as in Jerusalem, there are also people who stiffen their necks and proudly dismiss the words of God; for them, too, the 'day of the Lord' is announced, on which all that is high will be brought down and made low (see Isaiah 2—3). Consequently, the hope of God's universal judgement implies evaluating one's own contribution to justice and righteousness.

## 2  Hope of rescue from a tyrant (the theme of 'the symbol of evil')

**Isaiah 14:1–15, 22–27**

The first verses of this passage (vv. 1–2) indicate the aim of some of its admittedly harsh statements: it is about the well-founded hope that the fate of God's people, subdued under a tyrannical superpower, will be changed. Isaiah 13 shows the universal dimension of God's judgement on the 'day of the Lord' and its effects upon this type of tyrant. Isaiah 14 adds a few glimpses of how the 'day of the Lord' affects other nations (v. 6) and reveals some of the motivations of the tyrant (vv. 13–14). Here is someone who wants to establish himself as unrivalled ruler: 'above the stars of God', 'sit on the mount of assembly', 'I will make myself like the Most High' (vv. 13–14). He even dares to displace God, as sitting 'on the heights of Zaphon', a mythological term for God's dwelling place, implies.

For the people of the ancient Near East, honour and remembrance beyond death have been fundamental elements of their integrity. Isaiah 14 declares that Babylon's integrity will be destroyed (vv. 10–14), as she herself compromised her integrity by her delusions of grandeur. And the harsh words about the death of Babylon's children (13:16, 18; 14:21; see also Psalm 137:8–9) might be comprehensible in the light of 14:21: the circle of harm and evil is not to start all over again.

The words against this symbolic tyrant are continued by specific references to Assyria (vv. 24–27). This continuation shows that Babylon in Isaiah 13—14 is a paradigm for different empires in different times. The one closest to Isaiah's time is mentioned next, Assyria. This train of thought appears already in Isaiah 10: other powers might be tools in God's hand, but when they set themselves up as absolute – even above the Lord, the universal king – they are judged themselves. Isaiah 36—37 will show how, in a specific event in history, haughty ridicule against Jerusalem and her God, the Lord, will lead to a spectacular downfall for Assyria and her army in her attempt to invade Jerusalem.

The verses at the outset (vv. 1–4), however, also show that this perspective on judgement of Babylon and her different incorporations will be experienced in the future by those in Judah and Jerusalem who have been reshaped by God's judgement themselves.

## 3 Hope of overcoming enmity (the theme of 'enmity and peace')

**Isaiah 19:18–25**

Many passages in Isaiah 13—27 concentrate on God and what he does among the nations. A universal and a theocentric perspective correlate with each other here. This is important, as this feature contributes to the central image of God as king in the book of Isaiah (6:5; 24:23). Yet, in the middle of these oracles against the nations there is one place where we encounter a glimpse of the inner state of nations and the outcome of God's judgement: arch-enemies come together in peace.

Assyria and Egypt were the main adversaries at the time of Isaiah. The prophet had to intervene severely and point to the Lord as Jerusalem's shelter, when leading officials tried to sort out whom they would rather rely on, Egypt or Assyria (see Isaiah 31—32 below). The vision in our reading today stands out in the midst of the other oracles, as it points to the worship and service of the Lord as the foundation for peace. It is noteworthy that the restoration of Israel does not come from its military superiority, but from God as their source of blessing, as they live peacefully with nearby Assyria and Egypt.

For contemporary readers, the military texts in the Old Testament are often offensive. But in many cases, these passages most of all reflect the terrible and violent outcomes of a human heart in autonomy and hubris (see Isaiah 14 above). So for the people of the Old Testament, it is not the challenges of war and violence that stand out, but the occasional hint that God does not confine himself to limiting the worst cases of violence and cruelty but seeks to change human hearts in order to establish peace. The present passage is one such glimpse into the all-transforming power of a ministry that has reconciliation among arch-enemies as one of its goals.

It is obvious here that God does not neglect dark situations. He deals with them and even 'gets his hands dirty' in order to overcome them. Yet, at the same time, one can find an allusion to the more fundamental change that is needed: a change of the human heart.

# 4  Hope of a life without death (the theme of 'salvation from death')

**Isaiah 25:1–12; 26:16–19**

Similar to wisdom literature in the Old Testament, where aspects of life are addressed from a more universal perspective on anthropology, epistemology and justice, Isaiah 24 also emphasises that the Lord is the king of the whole world (6:5) and, consequently, his universal reign will affect the whole world, namely as universal judgement: the wickedness of humankind has reached such proportions (24:5–6) that God's universal kingship (6:3; 24:23) can be lived out only by judging the whole world (24:1–3) from Jerusalem (24:23).

It must be stressed, however, that this view on the world with Jerusalem as God's residence does not exclude the possibility that besides Assyria (Isaiah 10; 37), Babylon (Isaiah 13–14; 21), Tyre (Isaiah 23) and Edom (Isaiah 34), even Jerusalem could be identified with the wasted city (24:10) in the present (see 1:21–31).

In the light of this perspective on the undetermined future of 'the day of the Lord', Isaiah 25 introduces the proper attitude, by which everybody – in Judah, Jerusalem or wherever in the world – could persist in the midst of judgement and, even more, could experience judgement as salvation. Readers of Isaiah can identify with the voice of the prophet in 25:1–5 and acknowledge God's judgement as his salvation for the oppressed, as God is 'a refuge to the poor' and 'a refuge to the needy' (25:4). While Jerusalem may be in view as the future place of salvation in the unspecific phrase 'this mountain' (25:6–7, 10), it is God's kingdom that is praised for his overcoming of oppressive people for the sake of the poor and needy (25:1–5) and for his care for all those who come 'to this mountain' (25:6–12). What had been expected of an ideal human king in Jerusalem (see Psalm 72), that he cares for the poor and protects his people, is transcended in God's reign: his meal (25:6) and his shelter go far beyond any expectation, as he protects even from death, which he swallows (25:7–8).

As Isaiah 26 makes clear, this day has not come in the presence of its readers, but these words serve to provide a means to cling to the Lord (26:16–19) and to the hopes related to him, even when his kingship is not yet complete and the hope in revival is yet to be fulfilled.

# 5 Hope for the vineyard and beyond (the theme of 'restoration')

**Isaiah 26:20—27:13**

This passage assures those present in Jerusalem of a shelter while God's universal judgement is carried out (26:20–21). This judgement is one that discloses the cruelty of mankind, from which nobody can hide anymore. Hence, God's judgement is his commitment for the oppressed, mistreated and overlooked. And as far as this final judgement is concerned, it will result in total annihilation of any evil power: as in many other cultures at that time, mythical language is used in order to describe a reality that cannot be expressed otherwise: the dragon-like figure of Leviathan (27:1) symbolises the dangerous sea as well as all chaotic forces in the universe that threaten life, righteousness and salvation (compare also Psalm 74:12–14; 89:10–11; Job 41:1–8).

In contrast to his judgement of chaos and all evil, the Lord devotes himself in loving care to his 'vineyard', Jerusalem (27:2–6). But as verbal parallels with 5:1–7 and the bitter questions in 27:7–9 reveal, this passage envisions God's care for Jerusalem *after* his judgement of her, which included her 'thorns and briers' (27:4) and his sending them into exile (27:8).

Consequently, there is hope for the inhabitants of Jerusalem, who face their own judgement, for the time when the Lord devotes himself again to Jerusalem in order to carry out universal judgement from there. This restoration will also encompass returning exiles from Assyria and Babylon respectively ('from the channel of the Euphrates', 27:12; those 'lost in the land of Assyria', 27:13) as well as from Egypt ('to the Wadi of Egypt', 27:12).

There is hope for a life beyond judgement in Jerusalem. But it is a life in which the experiences of judgement remain alive in the form of prayers (27:7–9). Additionally, there remains an ambiguous relationship between Jerusalem (27:12) and the 'fortified city' (27:10): how do these 'cities' relate to each other? Do both represent Jerusalem, before and after God's judgement? Or do they represent Babylon and Jerusalem in the final judgement – or both?

# 6  Hope of a new king
# (the theme of 'the messiah: future and present')

**Isaiah 31:1—32:8**

Prophetic proclamation is not simply an announcement of future events. Even where it occurs like this, it is also confrontation with God in the present. This applies to the 'vision of Isaiah' (Isaiah 1—39) in general and to this passage too. The challenge of the present passage relates to the issue for which the present addressees are summoned: placed within the pincers of Assyria (from the north) and Egypt (from the south), leaders are tempted to put their trust in one of them. But Judah and her leaders are called to 'turn back to him' (31:6) instead of seeking help in Egypt (31:1–3). Isaiah appeals to his audience and their basic attitudes, which raises the question of whether they are able to return at all, or can only keep going along the ways that lead to judgement, as there might be a change and restoration only beyond judgement.

This passage is also challenging with respect to what the addressees can expect of the future. It is said that the threatening superpower Assyria will decline (31:8–9) and a new king will rise in Jerusalem. But this is not entirely an announcement of salvation. What is said here of the future king means a rejection of the present one. It is only by the new king that the Lord's salvific reign will be transmitted to Judah. There is hope in a new future; but it is a future that will be accomplished through imminent judgement.

Finally, this passage is challenging with respect to the hope in a new king: Although he fulfils the expectations of a just king – he provides shelter (32:2) and ensures a just society (32:1, 5) – his reign includes deeper changes. They are changes in the inner being of the people, their perceptions and their heart (32:3–4). Moreover, all announcements of the future king lead into a bitter characterisation of the present (32:6–7).

As much as Isaiah's message sketches a bright future, it discloses all the more the dark present in which he and his audience live, and what they are to expect in the immediate future. As much as Isaiah's message 'disempowers' the superpowers of his times, even more he challenges his audience to trust in their God instead.

## Guidelines

The diverse passages of this week might be perceived as a journey into realms of hope. Everybody knows the importance of hope. It enables us to endure in difficult circumstances, to encourage others, to take up responsibilities in troublesome times, to keep calm when there is frightening chaos and to stir up when there is stubborn indifference.

These passages can be read as challenges to hope in the Lord under every circumstance, as he is the universal king. There is hope for those who live in a tyranny of arrogant and blasphemous dominion – be it a country, a company, a household – as God does not withdraw from his responsibility for the poor, the offended and mistreated (Isaiah 13—14). There is hope for those who endure among enemies, for there is a God who transforms routes of war into paths of peace and worship (19:18–25). There is hope for those who hunger for universal justice, for God will establish his universal kingship in justice so that not even death can overcome it (Isaiah 25—26). There is hope for those who experience God's judgement, as his anger lasts only for the blink of an eye, but his mercy lasts forever (Isaiah 27). There is hope for those lost in the midst of political turmoil, for God helps by evaluating the options and identifying himself with his people by appointing a new king (Isaiah 31—32).

The times and challenges have certainly changed, but God's love for justice, for the poor, the oppressed and the stressed remains, as does his kingship that challenges all hubristic powers in this world. So these passages may encourage us to ask what the basis for our hopes is, what we could endure, whom we can inspire, what kind of responsibility we are ready to take up in order to be light in this world until God's kingdom will be accomplished by the universal king who cares for the needy.

---

**FURTHER READING**

B.S. Childs, *Isaiah: A commentary (Old Testament Library)* (Westminster John Knox Press, 2001).

J. Goldingay, *Isaiah (New International Biblical Commentary)* (Hendrickson Publishers, 2001).

J. Goldingay, *The Theology of the Book of Isaiah* (InterVarsity Press, 2014).

H.G.M. Williamson, *Variations on a Theme: King, messiah and servant in the book of Isaiah* (Authentic Media, 2006).

# Sensing the divine: John's word made flesh

Andrew Mayes

Since the earliest times, the fourth gospel has often been characterised by commentators as the most mystical of the gospels. Cyril of Alexandria (150–215) hailed John's work as 'the spiritual gospel'. But in the next two weeks, we'll see that the fourth gospel is rooted in the dust, dirt and beauty of the earth. It brims with sensuality, alerting and activating our senses, both bodily and spiritual. It is pervaded by a physicality, a materiality, shot through with transcendence, teeming with divine life. We shall appreciate afresh the meaning and significance of the most outrageous of all Christian claims: the idea that the divine Word took flesh in Jesus of Nazareth. We will trace this theme through the fourth gospel, identifying and celebrating its sensuous, tactile character. In particular, we shall see how the evangelist invests the five senses with theological meaning – and we develop our 'sixth sense'! We start to explore what implications this has for the practice of Christian spirituality and what this suggests for contemporary ways of praying and acting. These reflections are drawn from my book *Sensing the Divine* (BRF, 2019).

In today's culture, we are increasingly removed from the natural world. Technology is distancing us from nature, keeping us at one remove (at least) from an immediacy of contact and touch with the physical world. We have inserted a range of electronic gadgetries between ourselves and our environs, which often turn out to be barriers fencing us off from the natural world. This journey through John's gospel will help us to reconnect with the ground beneath our feet. It will stimulate a re-engagement, a re-enchantment, with God's world, which is brimming with epiphanies. John will help us to recognise and welcome these, to rediscover theophany in our very midst. He will help us, indeed, to become fully human once again, activating afresh our senses and sensibilities.

Quotations are taken from the New Revised Standard Version.

# 1 Unleashing the senses

**John 1:1–18**

As John looked out from his writing desk, he surveyed the horizons. The dawn was breaking in the east, dispelling the gloom of night. The first rays of light were illuminating the hills. He glimpsed the turquoise Aegean Sea and enjoyed watching the unceasing movement of the incoming waves. His eyes alighted on the ribbon of the river Cayster, and the stunning Meander Valley. He was awestruck by the mountains that surrounded him, with their exposed rocks and cover of cypress trees. He looked down on the vineyards below, and the irrigated horticulture with its rich harvest of fruits of every kind. Looking up, he saw the bluest of skies, broken only by the occasional cloud. He felt the wind blowing on his face, rustling his parchments. As he surveyed the creation around him, below him and above him, he began to write:

*In the beginning was the Word, and the Word was with God, and the Word was God. He was in the beginning with God. All things came into being through him...*

John's timeless words were not written in a vacuum. They are not an abstract philosophical treatise. They are a hymn of praise, a poem that springs from a certain context. They refer to an environment, an ecology, which John saw with his own enquiring eyes. John goes on in his gospel to delight in the natural world, because he discerns the Word in every wave and every fold in the hills, in every leaf and bud. He goes on to see how the vine, the flowing water, the seed, the shepherd and lamb reveal God the Word. For John, the Word – the very instrument and tool by which God originated and shaped the cosmos – focuses its divine power and presence in the human life of Jesus.

John's gospel is literally *sensational*, brimming and overflowing with tangible signs. It calls us to discover a new *sensibility* – a fresh receptivity to insights through the senses. It challenges us to new *sensitivity* as we read the text –a readiness to receive God's stunning self-revelation to us. Let us return to our senses!

# 2 Spirituality and sensuality

John 2:1–22

When John lived in Ephesus, its sprawling population numbered about 150,000. One of the largest cities of the Roman empire, it functioned as a pivotal trade and administrative centre, as well as a focus of pilgrimage to Artemis. Its vast theatre seating 25,000 spectators (mentioned in Acts 19:29) and significant stadium fostered a rich and sensuous culture. Many temples testified to the multicultural and pluralistic nature of its society. All human life was here: traders and sailors, craftsmen and artisans, priests and prostitutes, sages and shopkeepers. Poverty and need coexisted alongside opulence and riches. In its vibrant slave market, men and women were traded to be used in mining, construction or domestic settings. A quarter of the city's population was composed of slaves: the city's wealth was underpinned by exploitation.

As John looked out on this multifaceted mosaic of human life, he drew a deep breath. His pen hovered for a moment above the page. Dare he commit to writing those words that had been drumming in his mind – as he tried to encapsulate the mystery of Jesus? Was it too much to affirm? Looking at the city below him, with its blend of sweat and fragrance, its maelstrom of human emotion and fleshly activity, his pen touched the parchment. There was no going back:

*And the Word became flesh and lived among us, and we have seen his glory, the glory as of a father's only son, full of grace and truth. From his fullness we have all received, grace upon grace.*

These words in the prologue to John's gospel – celebrating creation and incarnation, Word and flesh – announce to the reader what is to come. John knows that he is pondering a paradox. The one of whom he will write is at once 'from above' yet living fully here below. John will need to combine, somehow, the intimacy and ultimacy of Jesus, his transcendence and tenderness. His testimony will be at once sublime and visceral.

As you read the two episodes in John 2 in today's reading, become alert to the sensuous and the sublime, the visceral and the spiritual. Look at the details in your imagination, smell the scents and taste the wine. After that, ponder again: 'The Word became flesh and dwelt among us.'

# 3 Encountering the body of Jesus

John 19:1–16

Frequently, John directs us to the physicality and tangible reality of Jesus' own flesh and body. He is wearied and tired after his journey, with sweat on his brow; he thirsts and he is hungry (John 4). His fingers mark a sign in the dust of the ground (John 8). His mouth emits spittle, to be made into a healing paste (John 9). Jesus shelters from the cold winter weather in the covered Porch of Solomon (John 10). Tears course over Jesus' face (John 11). His feet are anointed by Mary at Bethany (John 12) as she pours fragrant perfumes over them, a sign preparing for the burial to come.

The passion narratives direct us to take seriously the very human body of Jesus, and to gaze upon its different parts. His breast invites the presence of the beloved disciple (13:23). His fingers dip the bread at the last supper (13:26). His head is crowned with thorns (v. 2). His head is bowed in death (19:30). His lips cry, 'I thirst!' (19:28). His shoulders bear the weight of the cross (19:17). His back is furrowed by scourging (v. 1). His side is pierced with a spear and blood oozes from the wounds inflicted (19:34). His physical body is stripped naked by the soldiers (19:23). As Pilate declares: 'Here is the man!' (v. 5); 'Here he is: the Man!' (*The Message*). This is no spiritualised gospel. It is a physical gospel. Jesus is tangible, palpable, visceral, material. Why does John emphasise this?

At the time of his writing, the infant church was plagued by two heresies. *Docetism* affirmed that Jesus' body only seemed to be human, and that his human form was an apparition. Christ was so divine he could not have been human, since God lacked a material body, which therefore could not physically suffer. *Gnosticism* believed that all matter is evil: the body is a prison which we need to escape from. Jesus did not really suffer on the cross. He is not really a man, but a demi-god.

So John is empathic. He directs our gaze to the real body of Jesus in the passion. Human red blood and haemoglobin courses through his veins. John tells us that this dusty God thirsts. He weeps. He bleeds. He dies. He shares our human condition completely, utterly.

# 4 A sixth sense?

John 17:1–25

John uses the word 'know' 109 times! It could almost be said that knowing represents a sixth sense in the fourth gospel – an awareness or intuition of the supernatural or divine. John would have known the famous text:

*The Lord created human beings out of earth… He endowed them with strength like his own, and made them in his own image… They obtained the use of the five faculties of the Lord; as sixth he distributed to them the gift of mind.*

ECCLESIASTICUS 17

What did John have in mind when he talks about 'knowing'? He stands in the Hebraic tradition. Knowledge comes through encounter and intimacy (see Genesis 4:1). In Hebraic thought, knowing is dynamic. It is about engaging, entering into relationship, personally experiencing God's world. Knowing is about responding to the divine. Steeped in the Hebrew scriptures, John understands that the active use of the senses plays a vital role in the development of our relationships with others, the world and the divine.

In the Hebrew scriptures, the organ of knowledge is the heart: 'I will give them a heart to know that I am the Lord' (Jeremiah 24:7). To know with the heart – this is not sentimental or emotional. It is holistic, discovering God at the very centre of our life, welcoming God at the core of our being, responding with all our God-given faculties and powers of understanding and will. This intuitive approach, personally involving, engages all our powers of perception and prayerful reflection. In biblical language, the heart represents the point where reason, will, temperament and sensitivity converge. For John, too, the heart is the very centre of the human, uniting the intellectual, emotional and volitional functions of the person. It stands as a potent symbol of the inner life that is embodied and incarnate. 'You have pain now; but I will see you again, and your hearts will rejoice' (16:22).

Jesus models this deep knowing. Closest to the Father's heart (1:18), he has made God known. He declares: 'Very truly, I tell you, we speak of what we know' (3:11). He longs that we experience for ourselves this sixth sense: 'This is eternal life, that they may know you, the only true God, and Jesus Christ whom you have sent' (17:3). As you read John 17 today, ponder the references to this kind of 'knowing'.

# 5 A sense of place

From the outset, John's gospel reveals an acute sense of place. To the disciples' enquiry 'Where are you staying?', he responds invitingly 'Come and see.' This summons resounds across the gospel. We are invited to share in a journey of discovery. We are invited in the fourth gospel to accompany Jesus as he traverses the land as a pilgrim and traveller.

John has a sharp eye, a fascination, for the details at the sites, keen attentiveness to physicality and environment. He tells us the well is deep and it is in a field (4:5–11). There is a lot of water at Aenon near Salim (3:23). Grass covers hills above the Sea of Galilee (6:10). Lazarus' tomb is a cave (11:38). The tomb of Jesus has a low entrance (20:5). We learn details about the Jerusalem temple: forecourts accommodate a range of animals (2:13–16); the porticoes of Solomon offer shelter in winter (10:22–23); the treasury is a suitable place for teaching (8:20). John takes us to visit the Bethesda, describing a pool near the Sheep Gate with five colonnades or porticos (a line of columns supporting a roof-like structure, 5:2). He tells us that the house of the High Priest has a courtyard with a fire in it (18:5–18). John records that Jesus was crucified at Golgotha, the place of the skull, located 'near the city' (19:13). Uniquely, he tells us that there is a garden close by, with an unused tomb carved into the rock (19:41–42). We even learn that there is an inviting beach on the shore of Lake Galilee (21)!

But this alertness to the local and the particular is set within a cosmic perspective – literally so, for when John speaks of the world he uses the word *cosmos*. For John, there is a paradox in this widest of settings. The world is the object of God's love: 'For God so loved the world' (3:16). John's prologue affirms: 'The true light, which enlightens everyone, was coming into the world. He was in the world, and the world came into being through him; yet the world did not know him' (1:9–10). Moving between intimacy and ultimacy, John invites us to appreciate the small details of place without losing a sense of the bigger picture – of cosmic dimensions! In the fourth gospel, Jesus is at once the dusty pilgrim and traveller traversing the land, and the very creator Word made flesh!

25–31 March                                                              99

# 6  A sense of time

John's gospel reveals a deep paradox about a sense of time. It begins at the very dawn of time: 'In the beginning'. Jesus talks of being with the Father 'before the foundation of the world', sharing glory together in the pre-existent mists of eternity (17:5–24). He says: 'Before Abraham was, I am' (8:58). Yet alongside this sense of timelessness, the gospel notes the significance of recognising time. Timing is important. At what hour was the centurion's servant healed (4:53)? And everything in the fourth gospel moves towards the fateful and redeeming 'hour'.

Celebrating the passage of time in four distinct phases, John wants to pace the reader. First, the gospel notes the passage of *days*. In the opening narrative, a succession of days tumble after one another, creating a growing sense of excitement and anticipation that something remarkable is beginning to happen. Time gathers momentum, an irresistible thrust forward (1:29–35, 39–43; 2:1). Throughout, there is attentiveness to *years, festivals and seasons.* John punctuates the narrative by reference to the annual pilgrim feast of Passover. During the ponderous last supper discourses we pause, become contemplative, and linger on every word, entering *stillness*. But then a fast-paced passion draws us into the very current of Jesus' self-offering, his journey into glorification: we are carried along and swept up into the action. The intensifying tempo sweeps the reader to the cross, drawn by an unstoppable, irresistible momentum of love into the very *hour* of glory. The hour of Jesus' passion is precisely the time that the Passover lambs are being slaughtered: 'christology and chronology are inseparable' (Mark Stibbe, *John as Storyteller*, Cambridge University Press, 1994, p. 182).

The fourth gospel calls us to an alertness to God's work, which can never be predicted or timed. Routine expectations and planning go out of the window: 'Do you not say, "Four months more, then comes the harvest"? But I tell you, look around you, and see how the fields are ripe for harvesting' (4:35). We must not limit God. Human traditions limited what could be done on the sabbath, a 24-hour period of enforced rest. But in the fourth gospel, Jesus will not be so confined: 'My Father is still working, and I also am working' (5:17).

# Guidelines

- How do you find yourself responding to the invitation to encounter the divine in the physicality of Jesus' ministry and passion? Are you intrigued, attracted or hesitant? Why? What does this tell you about yourself?

- What is your experience of the relationship between the physical and the spiritual senses? How is the Word dwelling in the physicality of your life?

- Do you think that docetism and gnosticism have their modern-day counterparts? How persistent do you feel the body/soul dualism is in today's practice of prayer? Have you noticed any recent changes?

- Take a walk in order to develop your sixth sense, your sensing of the divine. This can be in the beauty of creation, in a housing estate or industrial landscape. Leave your comfort zone. Rule nothing out. Become present to your environment. Let physicality lead to spirituality, the concrete to prayer, the seen world to the unseen. Through your physical senses, come to sense the divine. Shift perceptions.

- Practise the art of theological reflection. Ask yourself: where am I glimpsing God or feeling his presence? What things speak to me of the divine? Read your environs symbolically and look for elements that somehow represent the sort of God you believe in. Open up your awareness of the divine – a deep *knowing*.

- In today's frantic world, we lose a sense of time and place, of sacred space. Globalisation and standardisation mean we may become less attentive to the small picture, the local, the particular and the peculiar. How can we maintain an attentiveness to the local without becoming excessively parochial in outlook? On the other hand, how can we live in solidarity with suffering peoples in different parts of the earth, while remaining rooted in our own locale? What clues do you get from John's gospel?

- What are you learning from John's gospel about approaches to time? What strikes you as being most significant to your own life? In what ways do you mark and celebrate the passing of time – during the day, week, year? How do you find yourself responding to John's call, in the last supper discourses, to slow right down and enter contemplative mode? What difference might this make to daily living?

# 1 Touching infinity

This week, we explore God's world through the senses. In the accounts of Easter, there seems at first sight a contradiction in connection with the sense of touch.

*Noli me tangere*: 'Touch me not' (v. 17, KJV). The Greek present tense indicates an ongoing action in progress: 'cease holding on to me'. It strongly suggests that Mary has already begun an embrace or touch with Christ, but this cannot be allowed to go on indefinitely. It is best rendered: 'Don't grasp, don't clutch or grip me.' Or more bluntly: 'Don't clasp me possessively, let me go!' Jesus is on the loose. He, the transcendent one, can't be held down. In Matthew and Mark's account, he is off to Galilee. In John, he is off to heaven. There is no holding him down: she has to let him go.

'Put (*balein*, literally 'thrust') your finger here and see my hands. Reach out your hand and put it in my side. Do not doubt but believe' (v. 27). Thomas is permitted to explore with his very fingertips the sacred and scarred body of Christ. He is invited to touch in order to verify, identify, clarify. This resonates with Luke's account where, to prove he is no ghost or apparition, Jesus says, '"Touch me and see; for a ghost does not have flesh and bones as you see that I have." And when he had said this, he showed them his hands and his feet' (Luke 24:39–40). In John, Thomas is permitted to touch the very wounds of Jesus, in order to confirm his identity and continuity – that it really is the same Jesus he knew before, not a dream, now hailed as 'my Lord and my God!' But he will not keep on holding on. He will release Jesus!

# 2 Seeing sacramentally

Throughout the fourth gospel, Jesus is seeking eyes wide open. He begins his ministry with the summons, the invitation: 'Come and see' (1:39). We are summoned to look, to open our eyes wide. The imperative 'behold!' – 'Take a long look!' – is found from the Baptist to Pilate.

The challenge, then, of this gospel is to open wide our eyes, minds and hearts. Jesus calls us to be curious, inquisitive, enquiring – not only to look, but also to see. John plays with this theme in chapter 4. In Samaria, Jesus counters a fixation with physical things and leads his hearers into a radically different way of looking at the world. Twice over, the woman at the well is stuck on a literal and physical hearing of Jesus' words (vv. 11, 15). But Jesus wants to lead her from the physicality of the water to its sacramentality, and how it powerfully symbolises the gift of God. The physical water and the well speak to Jesus of humanity's deep thirst for things of the Spirit and God's gracious provision.

The disciples too are bewitched by a concern for physical things. They had gone into the town to buy food (v. 8). Upon their return, they urge him, 'Rabbi, eat something' (v. 31). 'But he said to them, "I have food to eat that you do not know about." So the disciples said to one another, "Surely no one has brought him something to eat?"' (vv. 32–33).

Jesus sees food as highly symbolic and sacramental. Later, he says: 'The bread that I will give for the life of the world is my flesh' (6:51). Here, he explains: 'My food is to do the will of him who sent me' (v. 34). He is not talking about a picnic brought to him. He is talking of the deep nourishment and sustenance that comes from moving within the Father's will.

Jesus wants to awaken the disciples to a new vision and a fresh way of seeing reality. He calls them to become wide awake to the possibilities God is opening up: 'Look around you, and see how the fields are ripe for harvesting' (v. 35). But he is not talking about Samaritan agriculture. The fields around them speak to Jesus of the growth of the kingdom and the spiritual harvest which has become imminent.

# 3  Hearing God's voice

**John 10:1–18**

In the fourth gospel, Jesus models listening to the Father. He can only share and reveal what he himself has heard from his Father: 'He testifies to what he has seen and heard, yet no one accepts his testimony' (3:32). He describes himself as 'a man who has told you the truth that I heard from God' (8:40). He is clear: 'The word that you hear is not mine, but is from the Father who sent me' (14:24). But Jesus also reveals a close listening to the other in John's gospel. He hears the cries of the hungry (John 6). Jesus hears about the needs of the moment as he listens to his mother at Cana's wedding (John 2). He listens attentively to the paralytic's story (John 5). He hears the sobs of Mary Magdalene and asks, 'Why are you weeping?' (20:15).

In chapter 10, the voice of Jesus summons us to risk and adventure: 'My sheep hear my voice' (10:27). As a shepherd, he goes before us: 'He calls his own sheep by name and leads them *out*' (10:3) – that is, out of the comfort zone, out from the security and safety of the sheepfold's enclosure, into the risky and potentially dangerous open fields of the countryside. We are given the image of Jesus as a shepherd striding across the hills: 'When he has brought out all his own, he goes ahead of them, and the sheep follow him because they know his voice' (10:4). Note three challenges:

- We need to attune ourselves somehow actually to hear the call of Christ.
- We have to listen amidst the cacophony of competing demands. Clamouring voices compete for our attention: 'All who came before me are thieves and bandits; but the sheep did not listen to them' (10:8).
- If we listen to Jesus, we must be ready for adventurous journeying, because he leads us *out*.

In her *Interior Castle*, Teresa of Avila beckons us to leave the room of noisy, talkative prayer. She suggests we try the door into the room of deep listening silence. In 'the prayer of quiet', we give God a chance to communicate with us. So a controlling approach to prayer ('I'm in charge here, *I'm* talking!') moves to the prayer of receptivity and becoming susceptible to God. This can be transformative – and it is all about listening.

# 4 Feeding soul and body

**John 6:1–34**

John's gospel invites us to 'Taste and see that the Lord is good' (Psalm 34:8). The narrative of Jesus' ministry begins with a party, a wedding festival (John 2). It ends with a delicious meal by the water's edge in Galilee (John 21). Reading the narrative of chapter 6, we are often quick, with John himself, to spiritualise the event of the feeding of the 5,000. But behind this story are actual pangs of hunger and painfully rumbling stomachs. Before we consider the awesome eucharistic references here, we need to get real about the actual situation of physical hunger.

The Galilee of Jesus' time suffered the double trouble of oppression and poverty. Lee writes: 'Galileans… were oppressed, dehumanised and looked down upon. Galileans were marginalised by foreign invaders and also by the Jerusalem temple-state...' (S.H. Lee, *From a Liminal Place: An Asian American theology* (Fortress Press, 2010, p. 47). The phrase 'Galilee of the Gentiles' (Isaiah 9:1) may not be a compliment – it means 'circle of pagans'. A semi-autonomous frontier region, it was exposed to the nearby foreign countries and ethnicities.

In this region of deep poverty, the Galileans were crippled by heavy taxes: both to the Roman occupier and temple taxes. At the time of Jesus, ordinary families were being forced to quit their ancestral landholdings, where they had lived for centuries, to meet these demands. But then they had to pay rent for what had been their own fields and homes; they became caught in a downwards economic spiral, becoming tenants in their own property. Tax and rent robbed the Galilean peasant farmer of two-thirds of the family income. Many were living at barely subsistence level, while the Greco-Roman culture in Galilee nourished the creation of an upper class, the social elites, who owned great homes and estates. It was a world of 'haves' and 'have nots'. Yes, there was real physical hunger in Galilee.

'Very truly, I tell you, you are looking for me, not because you saw signs, but because you ate your fill of the loaves' (6:26). But actual physical pangs of hunger do point to spiritual need, and the loaves point to eucharistic feeding. The bread we eat at the altar must always remind us both of human hunger and the physicality of the incarnation, of the Word made flesh.

# 5 Welcoming the aroma of heaven

**John 11:55—12:11**

John offers us an alternative Martha/Mary story. In Luke, Mary is the contemplative, sitting at the feet of Jesus, while Martha represents the active, busy preparing meals. In John, we meet Mary and Martha in connection with the sense of smell, but it is not the smell of cooking!

First, we encounter Martha, ever the practical one, at the tomb of Lazarus. Jesus had delayed his visit to Bethany and arrives after the death of Lazarus and his entombment. As he asks that the stone is moved away from the mouth of the cave-tomb, 'Martha, the sister of the dead man, said to him, "Lord, already there is a stench because he has been dead for four days"' (11:39). Her nostrils will be assaulted by the rancid, retching whiff of death, the foul odour and reeking stink of mortality.

In contrast, we encounter Mary as she offers Jesus an exuberant, extravagant, fragrant act of adoration. It borders on the scandalous and outrageous, for she crosses boundaries, not only anointing the feet of Jesus with expensive perfume but also wiping them with her hair. John adds the sensory note: 'The house was filled with the fragrance of the perfume' (12:3). Unfettered, a sweet scent from expensive aromatic oils fills the air and wafts into the nostrils. The profusion of the perfume pervades, permeates every corner of the house, drifts through the air and percolates through every level. It is a heady, intoxicating, life-giving aroma: the scent of eternity. Jesus welcomes her gesture both as a sacrificial act of honour (costing about £20,000) and as a sign that his body is soon to be buried. He will shortly be anointed in death, with a quantity of spices enough for 200 people (19:39–40): his risen body, meeting Mary Magdalene, will be steaming in a haze of fragrance!

This episode challenges us to offer worship that is costly, sacrificial. We are moved to 'give and not to count the cost'. We are summoned to offer worship that is generous and extravagant, holding nothing back: as sacramental and expressive as Mary's act of devotion. Indeed, might our worship arise like Mary's perfume filling the whole house with its fragrance – and have an effect way beyond the sanctuary?

# 6 Reawakening: life in all its fullness

**John 13:1–15**

We conclude by celebrating John's central message: encountering the Word, we are invited to taste life in all its fullness. In the fourth gospel, Jesus brings a truth that sets us free: it is liberating, empowering, releasing us from captivities and things that hold us down, so we can become fully alive in Christ. Discovering in the Jesus of the fourth gospel a human flourishing, a spiritual blossoming, we know we must share this with others. In his epistle, John sums up his tactile, sensory discoveries:

*We declare to you what was from the beginning, what we have heard, what we have seen with our eyes, what we have looked at and touched with our hands, concerning the word of life – this life was revealed, and we have seen it and testify to it.*

1 JOHN 1:1–2

'The glory of God is a human being fully alive!' In making this affirmation, Irenaeus might be summing up John's gospel, which he loved so deeply. In his gospel, John celebrates the life-giving, living God. In the Word made flesh, the divine presence becomes palpable, tangible, verifiable. The Word is discovered through all the senses.

John sums up his gospel in the words he places on Jesus' lips: 'I came that they may have life, and have it abundantly' (10:10). This is life in all its exuberance. The Greek word *perissos* means above measure, more than average, above the common, extraordinary, more than sufficient, with a surplus. The Amplified Bible puts it: 'I came that they may have and enjoy life, and have it in abundance, to the full, till it overflows.' Jesus offers life in its fullest measure, life that is full and good. *The Message* gives us: 'I came so they can have real and eternal life, more and better life than they ever dreamed of.' The New Life Version renders this: 'I came so they might have life, a great full life.' This is expressed so poignantly in Jesus' exhilarating first sign: the wine of Cana – luscious, intoxicating – is a sign of God's extravagant, overflowing love shown to us in Jesus, a love we are invited to plunge ourselves into and share with others. We share with others the invitation of Jesus:

- 'Come and see!' (1:39)
- 'Lift up your eyes!' (4:35)
- 'Listen to my voice!' (10:3)
- 'Come and eat!' (21:12)
- 'Reach out your hand and touch!' (20:27)

Indeed, we might say with Pilate: 'Behold, the man!' (19:5).

## Guidelines

- These days, we are sensitive to the difference between appropriate touch: respectful, honouring, ministering, reverent or inappropriate, invasive, exploitative, abusive. When do you think the use of touch is appropriate in the practice of prayer? How do you feel about praying with your fingertips?

- How is it possible to retrain ourselves to see the world sacramentally? What is your experience of prayer as a space and process enabling the shifting and enlarging of perceptions?

- Why is it, do you think, that Christians often prefer talkative prayer to listening prayer? What is your experience of what Teresa of Avila calls 'the prayer of quiet'? Where and how do you hear God?

- 'How sweet are your words to my taste, sweeter than honey to my mouth!' (Psalm 119:103). What does your God taste like?

- How can we ensure that the sacred meal of the Eucharist expresses a solidarity with those who go hungry?

- Place in a bowl fragrant fruits, or a collection of flowers, leaves or fresh herbs. Enjoy sharp citrus scents and subtle fragrances. Allow your nostrils to tingle! Read the Song of Songs 5:5–6, 13–16 slowly: 'I arose to open to my beloved, and my hands dripped with myrrh…' How would you describe the fragrance of Christ? Then read 2 Corinthians 2:14–15: 'But thanks be to God, who… through us spreads in every place the fragrance that comes from knowing him. For we are the aroma of Christ.' What kind of fragrance or scent do you bring to others? Conclude by silently and deliberately crushing one item to release its full aroma through its brokenness. Pray that you too may be broken and given for others in need.

- What contributes to your thriving and flourishing as a Christian? What erodes or undermines this? What positive, creative steps can you take in order to enjoy the divine life flowing into you more and more? In what ways are you presently sharing the good news with others, as John did?

---

**FURTHER READING**

Yael Avrahami, *The Senses of Scripture: Sensory perception in the Hebrew Bible* (T&T Clark, 2012).

R. Alan Culpepper, *Anatomy of the Fourth Gospel: A study in literary design* (Fortress Press, 1959).

Andrew D. Mayes, *Holy Land? Challenging questions from the biblical landscape* (SPCK, 2011).

Bruce E. Schein, *Following the Way: The setting of John's gospel* (Augsburg Publishing House, 1980).

Ann Roberts Winsor, *A King is Bound in the Tresses: Allusions to the Song of Songs in the fourth gospel (Studies in Biblical Literature)* (Peter Lang Publishing Inc., 1999).

1–7 April

# Women in Luke's gospel

Jill Duff

Luke's gospel contains a surprising amount of material about women. These stories are often unique to Luke and diverse in their context: the women appear in a much wider range of situations than the other gospels (rich, poor, older, younger). Luke also captures Jesus' 'throwaway' lines to women in the crowds at his crucifixion (23:28) or intimate words to a woman who is anointing him at a Pharisee's house (7:36–50). These beautiful accounts offer an insight into the heart and posture of Jesus towards women in his day: radically refreshing.

'Do you see this woman?' (7:44). Jesus places women centre stage as examples of love, faith, dedication and discipleship. Throughout history, women are often the first trusted with the gospel; they have often been at the forefront of the work of the Spirit in cultures, communities and the church. Added to this, women have a tremendous influence on the relational fabric that makes up society from the cradle to the grave.

In these notes, we will call out of the shadows the women who were part of Jesus's journey from conception to cross, and join those first witnesses to the resurrection on Easter Day. Perhaps in this time, our spiritual imaginations might be sufficiently expanded to 'believe the women… [even though] their words seemed to [us] like nonsense' (24:11)?

Quotations are taken from the New International Version (Anglicised).

# 1 Elizabeth

**Luke 1:23–26; 39–66**

In this well-known opening chapter of Luke's gospel, let's put the spotlight on Elizabeth rather than Mary. Have you noticed how Elizabeth's faith and pregnancy set the scene for Mary's visit from the angel 'in the sixth month' of her seclusion (v. 26)? Elizabeth is the yardstick not just of time but of faith.

'The Lord has done this for me' (v. 25). Elizabeth is certain that her pregnancy is entirely God's work – a godincidence not a coincidence. This will be the same for Mary – but with a whole new dimension of divine intervention! Elizabeth sees with eyes of faith.

And wonderfully, Elizabeth's rich seedbed of faith summons out Mary's calling (as 'the mother of my Lord', v. 43) and Mary's song (vv. 46–55). 'Blessed is she who has believed that the Lord would fulfil his promises to her' (v. 45).

We all need Elizabeths in our lives, especially at those vulnerable transition times when God is mysteriously doing a new thing in us: people who can 'welcome the kingdom from afar' and spot the earliest green shoots of the Spirit's springtime life.

Elizabeth is the first in our panoply of heroines in Luke's gospel. What made her so special? Quite simply this: Elizabeth believed in the promises of God. As Hudson Taylor pithily puts it: 'God has spoken his word, he means what he says and he will do everything that he has promised.' Elizabeth is the first of the New Testament prophets – she just needs to be in the presence of Jesus hidden in Mary's womb and she is filled with the Holy Spirit and prophesies: 'Blessed are you among women and blessed is the child you will bear' (v. 42). How reassuring must her words have been to the newly pregnant Mary, who had hurried away from Nazareth to seek comfort as she grows to accommodate her vulnerable new calling.

Who is your Elizabeth? Or to whom is God calling you to be Elizabeth today? I am inspired by the seventh-century Hilda, who was an Abbess of a mixed monastery near Hartlepool. One day Caedmon, the tongue-tied cattle herd, had a dream in which he could sing a heavenly song. When he woke up, he could still remember it. He told the foreman, who in turn told Hilda, who invited him to sing his heavenly song at the banquet. Caedmon became famous for 'singing the gospel in the local language'. Who can we inspire today, after the example of Elizabeth and Hilda, to sing their song? They may be tongue-tied, but the Spirit of God can unbind and enable people to hear the 'wonders of God in their own tongues' (Acts 2:11).

# 2 Women who loved and supported Jesus

Luke 7:36—8:3

Only recently did I realise that the chapter break at 8:1 dissects what Luke would have intended to be a seamless story of our first experience of the adult Jesus and his relationship with women.

First, we meet the unnamed woman who 'had lived a sinful life' (7:37). She finds her way into the shadows at a very male-dominated gathering at Simon the Pharisee's. She is trying to stay hidden: 'As she stood behind him at his feet' (7:38). Weeping, wiping his feet with her hair, she has been muted. She is not welcome in this culture and yet her love for Jesus compels her in.

You can sense the squirming and embarrassment at this woman who is gatecrashing Simon's party. But wait for it… there are five words that shake the whole story, shatter the narrow frames that Simon and his Pharisaic culture have put around both the woman and Jesus: 'Do you see this woman?' (7:44) asks Jesus. It's easy to read Simon's thoughts: 'No, we don't want to see this woman… she's a prostitute and you're a half-baked prophet! But I'm too afraid of her to throw her out, she's cutting through all the social norms and pecking orders of a male society.'

No, Jesus is clear: she *loves* much – and she is pushing into the kingdom of God ahead of Simon (7:44–47). Jesus brings her out of the shadows and places her centre stage. He is undoing the work of the fall, which introduced a devastating brokenness in male and female relationships: 'He will rule over you' (Genesis 3:16).

For now, we still live in the shadow of the fall. But let's fill our lungs with the fresh air of his coming kingdom. Chimananda Ngozi Adiche (*Dear Ijeawele*, p. 37) writes: 'We have a world full of women who are unable to exhale fully because they have for so long been conditioned to fold themselves into shapes to make themselves likeable.'

Second, the passage closes with a beautiful cameo of the richer women who supported Jesus 'out of their own means' (8:3). As well as the twelve travelling with Jesus, there were women who were with him in their own right. They had been called out of the shadows ('cured of evil spirits and diseases', 8:2) and because they loved much, like the woman at Simon's house, they also gave much.

# 3 The bleeding woman and Jairus

Like other ancient biographers (e.g. Plutarch's *Lives*), Luke pairs characters together in the telling of his biography. But more radically, Luke always pairs a man with a woman: shepherd and woman with coin (Luke 1); Zechariah and Elizabeth (Luke 1); Simeon and Anna (Luke 2).

In this passage, Luke pairs Jairus, the synagogue ruler, with the bleeding woman. We are not told why she is bleeding – quite possibly after child-birth – but is it coincidental that she's been bleeding as long as Jairus's daughter has lived?

Jesus calls her out of the shadows and into the limelight (v. 45–46). And when no one comes forward first time round, he persists. The pivotal phrase in the passage comes in verse 47: 'Seeing that she could no longer go *unnoticed*'.

Jairus is used to be being noticed as the ruler of the synagogue; he approaches Jesus directly. But the woman is used to being *unnoticed*. In fact, her condition had led her to seek the shadows by law (Leviticus 12). Presumably, sheer desperation drove her to seek Jesus through a crowd so pressing that it 'almost crushed him' (v. 42).

What a curious pairing! The woman who wants to remain hidden is called out by Jesus, who publicly proclaims: 'Daughter, your faith has healed you, go in peace' (v. 48). Then even 'while Jesus was still speaking' (v. 49), the daughter of the well-noticed man dies: 'Don't bother the teacher anymore.' Both have been united in the posture that 'we shouldn't bother Jesus'.

In the face of this posture, what is Jesus' response? He persists (v. 50): 'Don't be afraid; just believe, and she will be healed.' People are forcing their way into the kingdom of God ahead of you (16:16). You might have thought that Jairus, the synagogue ruler, would be a forceful character. In fact, doesn't Jairus's position make him more likely to give up? Yes, it does. As we move into increasing positions of authority, the temptation to play safe and take care rises with increasing volume. I like Augustine's admiration of the Desert Fathers: 'These men have none of our education and yet they stand up and storm the gates of heaven.'

# 4  Mary and Martha

Martha starts well. If it weren't for Martha as networker, initiator, offerer of hospitality, then would Jesus have made this important friendship, which, in John's gospel, leads to the raising of their brother, Lazarus, from the dead (John 11) and Mary's anointing of Jesus for his death (John 12:1–11)? We need people like Martha who spot opportunities for the coming of the kingdom of God, and seize them.

But we are all familiar with the shadow side of Martha's can-do enthusiasm. 'Martha was distracted by all the preparations that had to be made' (10:40). And not only is there distraction in Martha's heart, but this manifests in moaning that Jesus doesn't care and jealousy that Mary has 'left me to do the work by myself' (v. 40). She is so cheesed off with Mary that she cannot even bring herself to speak with her directly. She *demands* that Jesus mediates: 'Tell her to help me!' (v. 40).

Does this sound familiar? When our tanks are empty, it's inevitable that we will find ourselves moaning, jealous and demanding. Perhaps most corrosive of all, we can perceive that Jesus doesn't care, that he doesn't answer prayer, so we had better get on with doing all the work ourselves – 'functional atheism'.

What is the antidote to Martha? Quite simply, it's modelled in Mary, who has 'chosen what is better' (10:42). If we are to sustain being on the frontiers, looking for the coming of the kingdom of God, we need to retreat into silence and contemplation in equal proportion to our frontline activity – like the mystics, like Jesus himself, who disappeared up the mountain when the crowd of opportunities were at his door (Mark 1:35–37). It can be so tempting to ride the adrenalin wave and keep going. But curiously, 'few things are needed – or indeed only one' (v. 42).

What would it mean for us today to follow Mary's example, who 'sat at the Lord's feet listening to what he said' (v. 39)? Can you consciously take time to centre yourself and 'seek his face' (Psalm 27:8): this was one of the most popular prayers in the early church. Do you know he loves your company? He's always pleased to see you. Listen to him now.

# 5 The crucifixion

Luke 23:26–56

As we journey with women in Luke this week, we reach Jesus' darkest hour. Notice how the women who had come with him from Galilee *stayed* with him and mourned (vv. 27–28, 49, 55–56).

An instinctive human reaction to pain is to run and hide – from our own pain and that of others. We see this in the response of the disciples when Jesus is arrested; we see this in my hymn book – there is no section for Good Friday, just a couple of hymns from Isaac Watts.

Pain threatens to bring chaos into our ordering of the world. Bereavement unravels the boundaries containing fear and pain. In what must have been his last selfless words before he is crucified, Jesus empathises with the oncoming tide of pain sweeping these women: 'Daughters of Jerusalem, do not weep for me; weep for yourselves and for your children' (v. 28).

From the start of creation, we see God working to put boundaries on chaos. In creation itself, he separates day from night and waters above from waters below. After the exodus, he gives the Israelites laws of purity to separate the unclean from the clean.

And yet the crucifixion is the axis on which the whole of creation turns. To avoid our pain is never to know that the cross of Christ offers the deep, deep centring that becomes wordlessly and mysteriously the foundation for all our questions, confusions and anguish.

Knowing you're not alone in pain is such a great gift. The women from Galilee stayed with Jesus; they were there throughout his crucifixion, at his death and in his burial; they took the initiative in ensuring that his dead body was well cared for, preparing costly spices and perfumes.

# 6 The resurrection

Luke 24:1–12

'He is not here; he has risen!' (v. 6).

Who was trusted with this epoch-shattering, universe-changing news? It was a group of women (v. 10). In fact, Mary Magdalene is the woman named as the witness to the resurrection in all four gospels. Her credentials? She had seven demons cast out of her (8:2). Those who are forgiven much love much (Luke 7). This is fully in keeping with Luke's sweeping story, sometimes termed the 'great reversal'.

It is also fully in keeping with the sense that God always keeps his promises: he *had said* this would happen: 'Remember how he told you…' (v. 6). This bookends the gospel with Elizabeth in 1:45: 'Blessed is she who has believed that what the Lord said to her will be accomplished'.

When did the angels appear? In the hidden place, when the women were due to be engaged in lowly tasks – lovingly embalming the body of their dead friend (v. 1). It's also in the hidden place that we see the first miracle in John's gospel: only the servants know where the water turned into wine has come from – not the master of the banquet (John 2:9).

'But they did not believe the women, because their words seemed to them like nonsense' (24:11). What are you believing that seems to others like nonsense? You will be in good company – remember Simeon and Anna (Luke 2) who saw a tiny spark of hope as the start of the dawn breaking in from on high. One of my heroines is Joan of Arc, who 'welcomed the future from afar'. She had a deep-seated sense that it was wrong that the English army had annexed such swathes of French soil during the Hundred Years' War. She prophesied and fought with the troops, and was burnt at the stake as a witch. But 22 years after her death, she was fully pardoned by the Pope and there was not a single English soldier left in France.

## Guidelines

- Is it time you asked Jesus to call you out of the shadows? Do you know you are loved much?

- Take time to ponder which character in the Luke 8 story you most relate to, regardless of your gender:

  - Jairus, with positional power, is happy to approach Jesus in public. But, when facing defeat or disappointment, is the posture of your household 'Don't bother the teacher anymore'? Do you default to 'functional atheism': death is beyond the scope of Jesus the teacher?

  - The woman is determined to go unnoticed. Perhaps this is the most significant healing Jesus can offer: overcoming not just the physical barrier (perhaps her bleeding was the excuse), but the internal posture that discounts yourself as a *daughter or son* of God. Does Jesus need to call you out of hiding today?

- Ponder and pray: who can you be with in their pain today? Or can you dare to invite the Spirit of God to highlight where you are running away from pain? Let Jesus minister to you – his hands still bear the scars of his crucifixion.

- All through Luke's gospel, women have been cast as visionaries, early-adopters, spotting signs of the coming of God's reversed kingdom in the secret places. Is it time for you to 'remember how he told you' (24:6)? What promises of God does he want you to welcome from afar today? Ask the Spirit to draw your eyes to horizons in your life, community, world, where the dawn from on high is breaking upon us (1:78).

- In Luke's 'great reversal', women are some of the key agents who Mary prophesies about in her Magnificat (1:46–55): '[He] has lifted up the humble. He has filled the hungry with good things.' Their very humility enables them to forcefully advance the kingdom of God (16:16). Where would you like to see the kingdom of God forcefully advancing in this Easter time?

- Why not take time with Mary to sit at Jesus's feet listening to him, to reach out to touch the hem of his garment, to sing with joy at the first inkling of his promises coming true like Elizabeth and Mary Magdalene?

# A week in the life of Jesus

## David Spriggs

The gospels devote between a quarter and a third of their words to the last week in the life of Jesus. This reminds us there must be a myriad of events, encounters and stories that we don't know – because every week of his ministry was as long as this one and even this has many hours about which we know nothing. But the more obvious point is that all the gospel writers consider this a critical, incisive and revealing week to which we should give close attention.

Our purpose in looking at some of these events and stories is not to reconstruct the chronology of the week or to reconcile the various gospels to one another. Rather, we will focus on a few of the encounters which show Jesus dealing with incredible pressure. Jesus' ministry was always under scrutiny: from the crowds, his disciples and, above all, those who saw in him a threat. One of the inevitable consequences of leadership is that we will come under pressure. How leaders handle pressure is revealing – whether it is Julius Caesar, Wellington, Queen Elizabeth II or Angela Merkel. We will be seeking to understand how Jesus coped with the vicious pressures of this week and try to learn something for ourselves.

Unless otherwise stated, quotations are taken from the New International Version (Anglicised).

15–21 April

## 1   Public opinion

**Mark 11:1–10; John 12:12–16**

Every leader these days needs to 'manage' public opinion. If there is some kind of scandal, whether in the local congregation or at a national level, the Christian leader needs to know how to manage the media. This will be to minimise damage to the 'reputation' of the church but also to minimise the pressure and the work.

Jesus was aware that he needed to manage public opinion too. On another occasion, when his actions had fuelled messianic speculation and the crowd threatened to make him king forcibly, he 'withdrew... to a mountain by himself' (John 6:15). Now he faced a similar challenge, but he couldn't go into hiding.

If these two accounts of the triumphal entry are read together, we see that Jesus was 'trapped' in a pincer movement. According to Mark's and Luke's accounts, those behind Jesus who had journeyed from Jericho to Jerusalem, or joined as pilgrims en route, had witnessed two amazing miracles. They had seen a blind man's sight restored and they had learnt that Zacchaeus, a chief tax collector in the lucrative oasis town of Jericho, had been saved and given away much of his fortune to the poor. The blind receive their sight and good news has come to the poor!

But the other crowd, coming from Jerusalem (which is John's perspective) were equally fired up with messianic anticipation as this was Passover time, the time of God's great deliverance. The time when a chair would be left vacant for the return of Elijah (or the Messiah). Hence, Jesus was trapped by two crowds of messianic anticipation – all focusing on him.

How then did Jesus deal with these supercharged crowds? Rebuke them? Dismiss them? Threaten them? No. He wisely sought to rechannel their energy. And he did it not with a war of words but through potent symbols, which clearly stayed in the popular imagination. Yes, as Messiah he would ride into Jerusalem. So the crowds got the message and joined in. As the pilgrim psalm indicated, they came 'with boughs in hand' (Psalm 118:27) and joined in 'the festal procession'. But he also took charge of the meaning of this procession by riding on a young, untrained donkey, to indicate that his messiahship was radically different to their expectations. Thus he posed a paradox that only the coming seven days would unravel. Would people choose the true Messiah or prefer their own construction?

# 2 Institutional authorities

**Mark 11:12–19, 27–33**

Jesus tried to avoid direct and overt clashes with the institutional elite in Jerusalem, until it became necessary. They had sent people to spy on him and to entrap him, both for what he said and what he did. On the whole, Jesus managed to sidestep their strategies. But now he had, in going to the temple area and ransacking the animals being sold for sacrifices, as well as by exposing the corruption inherent in the system, essentially issued a direct challenge to the institutional leaders of the nation. The very raison d'être of the temple system was being undermined. The Pharisees were mightily suspicious of Jesus, but the chief priests and elders represented the ruling elite (see Mark 14:53, 55). It was they who managed the primary institutions of Jerusalem and who had successfully kept their superior places in the hierarchy while, to their credit, protecting the nation from Roman aggression and even winning concessions for the Jewish people.

The disruption of the temple was a challenge they could not ignore. Jesus needed to be silenced. So they 'began looking for a way to kill him, for they feared him' (v. 18). Remarkable, isn't it? They were so powerful; they had their own militia at their disposal; they also had direct access to the Roman governor and, through him, the whole might of Roman rule. Yet they 'feared him'! Like a deadly virus, they didn't know how to handle him and they were afraid he could destroy them. So they attempted to discredit him or gain evidence they could use for a 'blasphemy' charge.

They asked Jesus, 'Who gave you authority to do this?' (v. 28). If he said 'God', that would be blasphemy. If he said 'my authority', that would mean they could accuse him of usurping God's place.

Jesus turned the tables by agreeing to answer their question if they answered his. He asked them whether John the Baptist had divine or merely human authority. They answered, 'We don't know.' Their reason is even more interesting: 'They feared the people' (v. 32). There was no democracy but they still feared the people.

Jesus was able to outflank these very powerful opponents because he knew that they were vulnerable. They valued their position, status and perks so much they were afraid both of the people directly and of Jesus' popularity and the damage he might cause. In contrast, Jesus had such a deep trust in God and held on to his human status so lightly that he was free.

## 3  Religious leaders

Mark 12:13–27

In Mark 3:6, there is a very ominous verse: 'The Pharisees went out and began to plot with the Herodians how they might kill Jesus.'

Now, for the second and only other time, we meet the Herodians. The Herodians and the Pharisees were in opposition about almost everything, other than their commitment to get rid of Jesus, for he threatened both ideologies. The Herodians favoured the dynasty of the Herods, whom the Pharisees regarded as impure and hence a severe threat to the coming of the messiah. This was the purpose of their attempt to meticulously obey the law and to get the Jewish people to do so wholesale: a necessary precursor, in their minds, for the coming of the messiah.

Both, however, wanted to remove Roman rule – indirectly or directly. So the question about paying taxes to Caesar was one they were probably united on. Perhaps they anticipated that they could lull Jesus into a false sense of security. Could not all three of them agree that paying taxes to Caesar, and thus implicitly accepting (or at least acquiescing) to Roman rule in Judaea and Jerusalem, was inherently wrong? What else could all this teaching about the kingdom of God mean? If it was alright for the Pharisees and Herodians to collude over this, surely Jesus could happily join this 'club'?

However, if Jesus were to agree with them, they could go to the ruling elite – notice that Mark says, 'they sent' them (v. 13), by which presumably he intended us to understand the chief priests and elders. Then they could report to them that Jesus rejected Roman rule and was therefore a threat to Rome. This would be a claim that Pilate would not be able to dismiss or ignore. Then they would have Jesus trapped – culpable of rebellion and warranting the death penalty. Job done.

Jesus might well have welcomed the opportunity to make friends with them and avoid yet more pressure. But he sees the trap. Jesus was not fooled either by their flattery (v. 14) or their hypocrisy (v. 15). His use of the coin reveals to them that they have already surrendered to Rome – they use its money!

# 4 Political leaders

**Mark 15:1–5; Luke 23:1–12**

Often, religious leaders and political leaders join forces and this puts increased pressure on those who seek to lead Christian congregations. This has happened in India, where Hindu priests and local governors decreed that seeking to convert people to Christianity was against the law; it has happened with Muslim clerics and their political allies; it has happened with Christian leaders and their state counterparts, for example the Orthodox

Church in some countries and historically even the Church of England inciting Parliament to persecute dissenters. This day in the life of Jesus makes it clear that this is nothing new.

Having determined to get rid of Jesus and organised a surrogate trial, the chief priests and the Sanhedrin send Jesus to Pilate hoping that he will sign off their death warrant. Interestingly, the first charge they bring against Jesus relates to yesterday's issue – that of paying taxes to Rome. Of course, Jesus had avoided implicating himself in such a position, which could be construed as rebellion. But who cares about the truth when the powerful want their way? This alerts us to the need for real discernment when we are told of religious leaders being accused of misdemeanours, whether of sexual or financial abuse.

Pilate chooses not to tackle Jesus about this issue but addresses the more serious charge of claiming to be a king. Clearly, Pilate is not impressed with Jesus' accusers and tells them he finds no reason to condemn him. He is delighted when they give him an escape clause, as he learns Jesus is from Galilee. This means he can send him to Herod. Normally, Pilate would not wish to affirm Herod's authority in this way – but expediency rules! And so the fiasco of legality continues as Pilate twists and turns to avoid responsibility.

Jesus finds himself in a situation where neither the truth nor justice (natural or political) count for much at all. He has no power of his own in these circumstances. How does Jesus cope with this pressure? We are not given many clues.

John, however, supplies us with the necessary insight. Jesus answers Pilate's claim to power by saying, 'You would have no power over me if it were not given to you from above' (John 19:11). He does not deny that Pilate has the power of life and death and he certainly does not show disrespect for Pilate's power, but his words indicate that he is still entrusting himself to God.

# 5  Friends or foes? – Peter and Judas

**Mark 14:10–11, 17–21, 26–31**

Colleagues, family members and close friends can sometimes become sources of intense pressure. Sometimes this is because they care for us so much that the thought of us going (voluntarily) into difficult or dangerous situations is too much for them to cope with, so they attempt to 'protect' us by seeking to divert us from the path we have chosen or from implementing decisions we know we need to take (see Mark 8:31–33). On other occasions, they add to our burden because they fall out with each other or show us they have not matured in the faith as we hoped (Mark 10:35–41).

In his final days, the disciples added pressure to Jesus' life in other ways. With Peter, it was partly his bravado. In spite of Jesus' warnings, he remained so sure of himself that he could not allow Jesus' words to help him when the crunch came. He could not absorb them and the reality about himself they indicated. So he collapsed under the pressure, adding to Jesus' burdens as he knew how this would devastate Peter. Jesus did everything he could to save Peter from his own worst self, including praying for him (Luke 22:31–32), but it was to no avail – or so it seemed at first. Jesus was working for Peter's eventual redemption and restoration even as he faced his own death. What an example!

With Judas, it was even more intense – the pain and sense of rejection that Jesus must have had to handle is almost unimaginable. Judas didn't betray him because he had somehow been cornered or was being blackmailed by the religious leaders. At the human level, he seems to have volunteered to ensure that Jesus could be captured and killed. Scholars have speculated about his real intentions and motives. The only clue the gospel writers give us is that somehow money was involved. Then the final hammer blow: Judas betrayed him with the kiss of friendship: 'So when he came, he went up to him at once and said "Rabbi!" and kissed him' (Mark 14:45, NRSV).

It is not too much to imagine that, for Jesus, the greatest pain and pressure was not that Judas betrayed him, not even the way he did it, but that Jesus knew the agony and desperation that Judas would go through after the arrest, trial and crucifixion. What an example!

# 6 Ultimate failure – Gethsemane and the cross

**Mark 14:32–42; 15:25–34**

It is clear that Jesus had lived with an awareness of his eventual 'fate' for many months, if not years – the many times he sought to prepare his disciples for the 'end' shows this. Awaiting an operation, living with the imminent anticipation of a loved one's death, preparing for a difficult meeting where we expect to be intensely scrutinised or oppressively criticised – these experiences give us a small clue as to the intense pressure that this must have brought to Jesus. We know that, for Jesus, this was balanced by an awareness of God's ultimate plan, but for a few weeks, he has been heading towards Jerusalem with the knowledge that this would culminate in his death.

How did he cope? One way we might deal with this kind of pressure is to push it to the back of our minds or pretend to ourselves it's not going to happen. Another is to make a 'bucket list' and fulfil dreams we have had for many years. Neither of these was Jesus' way! His way was to gather a small group of his friends and then to meet with God – perhaps as never before. We know it was Jesus' habit to take time out to pray with God. We may surmise that this well-trodden path of spiritual exercises stood him in good stead at this critical point. But it made these vital times no easier.

*[He] began to be deeply distressed and troubled. 'My soul is overwhelmed with sorrow to the point of death...' He fell to the ground and prayed that if possible the hour might pass from him.*

MARK 14:33—35

Such verses require us to pause and ponder deeply. What did it cost Jesus to utter the word 'Abba' in this setting?

It seems a trivialisation to say that when the cost of Christian leadership becomes really intense, deeply affecting both ourselves and those closest to us, then we do well to follow this example. But we do: facing up to the reality in the presence of God; affirming our trust through gritted teeth and tears whether of rage or perplexity; laying ourselves – with all our vulnerability – before him. Then eventually (and we have no idea how long this took Jesus or will take us), we come to the place where we can say: 'Yet not what I will, but what you will' (Mark 14:36).

## Guidelines

By means of our journey through Holy Week, we have focused on some of the many pressures Jesus had to handle. These readings provide us with a mirror for today's leadership pressures and thus a provocation to consider how fully we are following Jesus in this area of our lives.

This section invites us to walk prayerfully with Jesus through the pressures of leadership.

The triumphal entry is a masterclass in managing public expectations. Jesus refuses to avoid the challenges and neither does he surrender to popularism. Instead, through the use of culturally embedded symbols, he seeks to encourage the people to reconsider their expectations and commitment to him.

The next two days show Jesus handling the cunning ploys of his religious opponents, first the chief priests and elders and then the Pharisees and Herodians. Rather than allowing himself to be provoked into a public rebuttal or angry argument to defend himself, Jesus uses his deep awareness of human nature to enable him to sidestep their traps and potentially open their minds to a different way of viewing life before God.

The next two notes offer us contrasting situations. First, the vulnerability of coping with those in power who seem to have total control, and then the desperate isolation created by the failure and betrayal of our friends and colleagues. Jesus copes with both because he is not mesmerised by those in power nor deceived by those closest to him. Equally, he never takes his eyes off God and maintains his trust and obedience throughout.

Finally, we see Jesus fighting the battle with himself. Gethsemane and the crucifixion become times of total purification and surrender to God's purposes.

# Resurrection in Acts

Ian Paul

There are a number of interrelated themes in the Acts of the Apostles, and different commentators give these themes different prominence. As the title suggests, there is an important focus on the ministry of the apostles, both the eleven (expanded again to twelve) who were called by Jesus, but also a wider ministry of apostles beyond the twelve. At the heart of the narrative are the key leaders: Peter (apostle primarily to the Jews) and Paul (apostle primarily to the Gentiles). Luke makes sure that his account gives equal importance to both, with each of them preaching, experiencing opposition, performing remarkable miracles, being imprisoned and released, and being instrumental in the spread of the message about Jesus.

A second focus is the work of the Spirit – and some might argue that the book should be called the Acts of the Spirit rather than the Acts of the Apostles! It is the gift of the Spirit at Pentecost which sets the context for the whole narrative; it is the Spirit who enables the 'signs and wonders' that marked the apostolic ministry; and it is the Spirit who equips his people for their courageous testimony. The Spirit is at times the stage manager of the drama, as the ministry and testimony spreads out in widening circles, like ripples in a pond, so that the story that begins in a marginal province of the Roman Empire ends with the message being taken to that empire's centre and proclaimed unhindered.

Yet undergirding all this action is a core message, which is less often the focus of commentary but which holds all the other things together: the message of Jesus' resurrection. It is the resurrection (followed by Jesus' ascension) which makes possible the outpouring of the Spirit; by the resurrection, God vindicates Jesus and proves that he was the promised Messiah; the resurrection both fulfils the promises of the past and holds out hope for the future; and the resurrection puts all beliefs and philosophies under scrutiny. Through the many and varied episodes of Acts, the resurrection features with remarkable consistency – as we will discover in the coming days.

Unless otherwise stated, quotations are from the New International Version (Anglicised).

# 1 The resurrection forms a new community

**Acts 1:1–22**

The opening chapter of Acts is key in setting the scene for all that follows. Luke points us to three particular themes in his brief description of the 'in-between' time of '40 days' (v. 3), recalling both the 40 years of desert wandering in Exodus and Jesus' preparation time of 40 days in the desert on the same pattern.

The first theme is that of *continuity*. Luke has already written to Theophilus of all that Jesus '*began* to do and to teach' (v. 1) and is now going to describe Jesus' continuing ministry through his followers in the power of the Spirit. Jesus continues to teach 'through the Holy Spirit' (v. 2) and Luke draws some detailed parallels to the work of the Spirit from his gospel. Just as the Spirit 'came on' Mary in Luke 1:35, enabling Mary to testify to God's goodness and bringing to birth the Messiah, so the Spirit 'comes on' the disciples (v. 8), enabling them to testify and bringing to birth a new community of followers of Jesus.

This continuity is also expressed in the repeated emphasis on *community*. They listened to Jesus' teaching and asked him questions 'gathered around him' (v. 6), and this community included the remaining eleven of the twelve disciples (compare Luke 6:12–16) as well as the women who accompanied Jesus (Luke 8:1–3) and now Jesus' own family, who had previously been at a distance from his ministry. As they consider the need to appoint a successor to Judas Iscariot, it becomes clear what defines this community. They are seeking someone who has had continuous experience with them of this Jewish renewal movement starting with John the Baptist – but the defining feature is that this person must be 'a witness with us of his resurrection' (v. 21–22). This renewal of God's people focuses on a resurrection community – as Paul confirms in his account in 1 Corinthians 15:3–8.

This is what makes the third theme so important – that of *confidence* in their resurrection message. Why does Jesus spend so much time with them prior to the ascension? So that he could present 'himself to them and gave many convincing proofs that he was alive' (v. 3). This deep confidence will allow the resurrection community to testify and minister in continuity with Jesus' own ministry in the face of serious opposition.

# 2 The resurrection calls for repentance

Acts 2:14–39

Pentecost is sometimes called the 'birthday of the church', and, as we have seen, Luke has drawn a parallel between the birth of Jesus and the birth of this new movement. But the word translated 'church', *ekklesia*, was used in the Greek Old Testament for the 'congregation' of Israel, the people of God. Luke does not see 'the church' as replacing 'Israel' but depicts this new movement as a fulfilment of God's promises and the people's hopes.

Luke's version of Peter's speech explaining the dramatic events of the Spirit's outpouring falls into two halves of equal length – verses 14b to 24, and 25 to 36 – and some scholars argue that the text has 444 syllables in each half, making 888 in total, the number of Jesus' name in Greek. The speech clearly focuses on Jesus and ends with the rousing climax: 'God has made this Jesus, whom you crucified, both Lord and Messiah (or 'Christ')' (v. 36). Peter reaches this conclusion in each half, moving from Old Testament texts, seeing them fulfilled in Jesus and finding full expression in his resurrection.

First, the outpouring of the Spirit, which the crowd have witnessed in the sound of wind, the tongues of fire and the multilingual praise of God, fulfils Joel's prophecy of the 'last days' (v. 17–21). The 'signs and wonders' Joel had anticipated has already begun in Jesus' ministry, and Peter assumes that many in the crowd are already aware of this. These reached their fullest expression when 'God raised [Jesus] from the dead' (v. 24), an event for Peter's hearers of both national and cosmic significance, since resurrection meant both the renewal of Israel (Ezekiel 37) and the end of the age (Daniel 12:2). Second, Jesus' victory over death fulfilled King David's hope for life with God, which David did not himself experience. David saw 'what was to come' (v. 31) not in a wooden, literalist sense – but in the sense that he knew that God was faithful and would triumph over death, and this was now achieved in Jesus' resurrection.

The resurrection changed everything, and demonstrated God's vindication of Jesus which completely overturned his rejection and condemnation by the Jewish authorities. Just as at the start of Jesus' ministry (Mark 1:15), a new reality has broken in – and the only appropriate response is to repent and believe.

# 3  The resurrection overturns the old order

The signs and wonders that are the hallmark of the presence of the Spirit, in fulfilment of Joel's prophecy, have continued as Peter and John heal the lame man by the Beautiful Gate in Acts 3. Just as Mary had proclaimed in the Magnificat (Luke 1:46–55), God's presence in power means that the humble are 'lifted up'. But it also means that the rulers are 'brought down', and this explains the sudden shift in focus as the two disciples are held ('jail' was a place of holding for trial, rather than punishment) and then quizzed by the leaders.

The size of this new movement is not yet the concern of the authorities; what they are worried about is the content of its teaching. Luke notes that the Sadducees 'who say there is no resurrection' (Luke 20:27) are the first to be concerned, along with others whose influence comes from their link with the temple and the sacrificial system. Luke has already linked his whole story with Annas and Caiaphas (Luke 3:2) and the other gospel writers note their role in Jesus' trial (Matthew 26:57; John 18:24). Peter and John are facing the same challenges that Jesus did, and cite the same prophetic psalm (Psalm 118) as explanation for what God is now doing. Jesus is 'the stone you builders rejected' who is now 'the cornerstone' (compare Luke 20:17), and this language of stones and buildings offers a direct challenge to the importance of the temple.

Peter makes a direct link between the resurrection and the power to heal; just as Jesus was raised up from death to stand before God, so this man has been raised up from his lameness to stand; both are a demonstration of God's action. But he goes further: if God really is rebuilding his people on the foundation of Jesus (1 Corinthians 3:11), then the world has changed. Joel's prophecy makes it clear that everyone who 'calls on the name of the Lord', that is, Israel's God, 'will be saved' (Joel 2:32), but Peter now claims that this Lord is none other than Jesus (compare Romans 10:6). The resurrection not only offers the forgiveness of sins and releases the power for healing by the Spirit, but it signals the end of the old age and the new age of the longed-for kingdom breaking in. No wonder the authorities were worried!

# 4 The resurrection as the centre of testimony

**Acts 4:23–37**

In this next part of Acts 4, the themes of continuity, community and confidence (that we saw from Acts 1) are once again prominent. Just as Jesus' rejection by the leaders continued the experience of prophets of the Old Testament (Luke 13:34), so the opposition that Peter and John are experiencing continues the rebellion of the leaders of the nations against God's just rule in Psalm 2. In the face of this, their knowledge of Jesus' resurrection gives them ever more confidence; instead of praying for protection (as many of us might), they ask for greater boldness!

This is all in the context of a radical commitment to community, extending not just to common practices of worship and teaching, but to shared financial resources too. In the summary statement of verse 32, Luke seems deliberately to be echoing his earlier summary in 2:44–45, but expands on what that means in more detail, as individuals sell their possessions and share the proceeds. This leads to the positive example of Joseph Barnabas, who becomes key in the beginnings of the Gentile mission with Paul, and the negative example of Ananias and Sapphira in the next chapter. It seems that this new communal life of the Spirit, centred on the resurrection, brings the division of judgement as well as the unity of a shared life.

But at the centre of all this lies the word of testimony. Testimony (or witness) is the thread running right through the narrative of Acts. At the beginning, Jesus promises the gift of the Spirit so that 'you will be my witnesses' (1:8) in ever-increasing circles from Jerusalem outwards; at the end, Paul is continuing to bear witness as he preaches about Jesus unhindered (28:31). (This is one of several ways that Luke and Acts are surprisingly connected with the book of Revelation, where faithful testimony is also a central theme.) As the believers prayed for boldness and were filled with the Spirit, they 'spoke the word of God' (v. 31) – the message about the resurrection (compare 4:4 and 8:25). Similarly, the power of the Spirit enables the apostles (here meaning the twelve) to 'testify to the resurrection of the Lord Jesus' (v. 33). The resurrection gives them a new communal life, a new committed purpose and a new central message.

# 5  The resurrection as the fulfilment of the story of Israel

**Acts 5:27–32; 7:35–38**

If this message about Jesus and the resurrection is bringing in a whole new order of things, there is a serious theological question: is this 'new order' really something of God, or is it leading people astray? Is this new community displacing the 'congregation of Israel' that God led through the wilderness into the promised land? If these apostles have a new message, is it contradicting what God has taught them? Moses himself warned against new teaching – even if the messenger was able to do 'signs and wonders' (Deuteronomy 13:1–3). The problem of 'another teaching' is one that Paul had to face early on (Galatians 1:6–9), and it is one that faces every generation of Christians.

In Acts 5, Peter and the other apostles are once again before the authorities, following the healing of many and their own miraculous release from prison. Peter's defence has a triple emphasis on the story of Israel. First, it is 'the God of our ancestors' who has 'raised Jesus from the dead' (5:30); it is the living God, worshipped by his living people, who has brought life where there was death. This is characteristic of God from the beginning, when he breathed into the 'earth creature' (*adam*) the 'breath of life' (Genesis 2:7). And it marks his relationship with his people, who find renewal in exile when the Spirit of God breathes new life into them (Ezekiel 37:10). Second, Peter is clear that the purpose of the resurrection and exaltation of Jesus relates to Israel – to bring them to repentance and forgiveness (5:31), the hope expressed at the start of Luke's whole account (Luke 1:77). Third, the signs and wonders of the Spirit are given to those 'who obey God' (5:32) – so the miracles are actually confirmation of the message as coming from God.

The accusation against Stephen is similar – that he is leading people away from the teaching of Moses. In response, in Acts 7 Stephen rehearses the history of Israel, and the turning point of his speech centres on Moses himself. He was rejected as leader by the people; God vindicated him; and the signs and wonders he did confirmed this. Jesus was rejected in the same way, but God vindicated him (in the resurrection) and the signs and wonders done by Stephen confirm that this message is from God.

# 6 The resurrection as boundary-breaking

Acts 10:34–46

The first part of Acts has focused on the message in Jerusalem and to the Jews there, and has begun to see the ripples spread out as predicted by Jesus in 1:8. The persecution of the fledgling community has resulted in them preaching 'the word wherever they went' (8:4), which has already led to some surprising results – the message being received by the despised Samaritans, and the Ethiopian eunuch coming to faith and being baptised. We have been introduced to Saul, who will proclaim God's name to the Gentiles (9:15), but he has yet to take centre stage.

In fact, the ministry to the Gentiles begins with Peter's change of understanding through the vision of the sheet with unclean animals, representing the 'unclean' Gentiles whom God now wants to reach. Peter's address is unapologetically particular, focusing on the events of Jesus' ministry, death and resurrection, and specifically mentioning Nazareth, Galilee, the 'country of the Jews' and Jerusalem, all in fulfilment of the 'prophets' who (together with the law) form the Jewish scriptures. And he gives a special prominence to the 'witnesses… who ate and drank with him after he rose from the dead' (v. 41). The resurrection forms a community of witness and, in doing so, forms a boundary distinguishing between those on the inside and those on the outside, just as Jesus' own teaching had done (see Mark 4:11).

And yet at every stage, Peter then moves across into universal language. The message from God to the people of Israel is that Jesus is 'Lord of *all*' (v. 36). His ministry involved delivering '*all* who were under the power of the devil' (v. 38). And in his resurrection, God appointed him as 'judge of the living and the dead' (v. 42), not just the judge of Israel. This then means that '*everyone* who believes in him', Jew and Gentile alike, will 'receive forgiveness of sins' (v. 43). The resurrection addresses not simply the hopes of Israel for a renewed national life, but the hope of all humanity that, in the words of David, 'I will see… the Lord in the land of the living' (Psalm 27:13). The resurrection is not just boundary-making, but boundary-breaking, creating a community that straddles divisions of race, nationality and ethnicity, centred on the testimony to the power of the God of Israel.

# Guidelines

We noted in Acts 1 that the resurrection offers continuity, forms community, and gives confidence. But it is already clear that it does these things in ways that we probably did not expect.

Peter and the apostles are emphatic that Jesus' ministry, death and resurrection are in complete continuity with God's plan for Israel and the world – and it could hardly be understood as anything else. From Matthew, through Paul, to the book of Revelation, Jesus is the fulfilment of all that God has done beforehand, the crowning and completion of his action, and the last Word of all the words of God. Yet it looks like a new and unexpected thing both to the Jewish leaders and to us – and perhaps even to the apostles themselves. Peter confidently claims that 'all the prophets [of the Old Testament] testify about him' (Acts 10:43), but you have to read the prophets in a particular way, and with the benefit of hindsight, to see that.

The resurrection also forms a community centred on those who spent the 40 days with Jesus prior to the ascension, and bounded by belief in Jesus as God's anointed judge through whom we have forgiveness. There is a very clear sense of division between those who join this new movement and those who resist it; indeed, Jesus had said his coming would bring division (Luke 12:51–52). And yet the boundaries of this community do not follow expected lines; it already includes many, like the Samaritans and the Ethiopian eunuch, whom many would have excluded, but excludes many, like the Sadducees and other Jewish leaders, whom many would have assumed included. This not about a sloppy 'anything goes' inclusion, since these people receive the gift of the *Holy* Spirit and are incorporated into the distinct and holy people of God.

And the resurrection gives this new community a sense of confidence – but a confidence that looks very vulnerable. They are persecuted and scattered, and God uses this communal fragility as a way of taking the message about new life in Jesus to unexpected places where it takes root and flourishes.

The resurrection not only challenges our expectations of what God is doing, but the way in which he is doing it. It is a work of God that we cannot replicate by our own efforts.

# 1 The resurrection shows the successor to David

**Acts 13:16–41**

The ministries of Peter and Paul have dovetailed in the last few chapters, with Paul's encounter with Jesus on the road to Damascus coming between episodes in Peter's ministry. But the commissioning of Paul and Barnabas by the Christians in Antioch (13:3) shifts the focus decisively to Paul. After the encounter with Elymas the sorcerer on the island of Cyprus, Paul and his companions land in Pamphylia, now the south coast of Turkey, and continue to preach the good news about Jesus and the resurrection.

Ananias was told that Paul would 'proclaim [Jesus'] name to the Gentiles' (9:15) and Paul himself confirms this in Galatians 2:7–8, contrasting his ministry with that of Peter's to the Jews. But here Paul follows his consistent practice on his travels – to go first to the synagogue and tell his message to Jews and 'God-fearing' Gentiles (vv. 16, 26) before then preaching to the whole population of the city (13:44) and seeing many Gentiles joining this Jewish renewal movement (13:48). This expresses Paul's belief that the good news is 'first to the Jew, then to the Gentile' (Romans 1:16). Like Peter, Paul 'motioned with his hand' to gain attention (v. 16; 12:17) and, like Peter at Pentecost, makes his appeal in a speech which has two halves (vv. 16–31 and vv. 32–41). And Paul agrees with Peter's emphasis on Jesus as the one pointed to by the prophets (v. 27).

But in a move of extraordinary irony, Paul's speech rehearses the history of Israel in the way that Stephen's had done before his murder, which Paul witnessed and of which (at the time) he approved. Paul shifts the focus from Moses to David, and from similarity to contrast. Jesus' resurrection is the fulfilment of the ancestral promise (v. 33) because it means that Jesus is the one who receives the promise that David did not see realised. Like the Davidic king in the royal Psalm 2, Jesus is the true Son of God. But, unlike him, Jesus has received the promise of transcending death through resurrection (v. 37), a promise that was intended for all the people of God (see Isaiah 55:3, which Paul quotes) and which would spill over to the nations of the world. The resurrection shows Jesus to be 'great David's greater son'.

# 2 The resurrection as challenge to culture (1)

We have jumped ahead to the middle of the second phase of Paul's missionary travels, moving beyond Asia (western Turkey) and into Europe. After visiting Philippi, Paul is escaping those pursuing him from Thessalonica, and he has arrived in Athens, on his way further south to the then more important city of Corinth. A striking aspect of this episode is that Paul is, for the first and last time, ministering alone. In both his teaching and his writing, he habitually works with others, but now awaits his co-workers Silas and Timothy. This does not prevent Paul from preaching, but it is no coincidence that this solo ministry is the least fruitful in Acts.

Luke describes the pantheon of Greek gods in typically Jewish terms – as 'idols' (v. 16). In the Old Testament, the description of other religions as idol worship expressed both the error and the foolishness of non-Jewish belief; the mocking description in Isaiah 44:9–20 contrasts idols with the uniqueness and the power of the God of Israel to rescue his people from exile. Paul's preaching strategy takes a significant turn here; as well as debating in the synagogue with Jews and the associated God-fearers as he has done before, he also now debates in the marketplace, engaging with those with whom he shares little in terms of religious and philosophical outlook (v. 17). The lack of mutual understanding is evident from their reaction, describing Paul as a 'babbler' (v. 18). The word derives from the action of birds who peck here and there at seeds, somewhat at random, and was used in mockery of those who did not have a proper philosophical system, but pretentiously threw out disconnected ideas.

The other criticism tells us why they thought this: Paul is 'advocating foreign gods' (v. 18). The term for 'resurrection' in Greek is the feminine noun *anastasis*, from which we get the woman's name Anastasia. Paul was so insistent on talking about Jesus and *anastasis* that his listeners understood this as a pair of gods, one male and one female. Despite the incomprehension and apparent irrelevance, Paul remains resolutely committed to the message of the resurrection as central to the good news he brings – offering the liberating truth to a culture ignorant of the reality of Paul's God.

# 3 The resurrection as challenge to culture (2)

Acts 17:22–34

Because of his debating in the *agora*, the main marketplace in the centre of Athens, Paul has been called before the council of the senior men governing Athens. They meet at the Areopagus ('Ares Rock'), a rocky hill overlooking the marketplace, to the west of the main acropolis on which the Parthenon was built. The implication is that Paul is making an appeal for recognition of his new gods, and the council need to grant approval for a new altar to be added in the pantheon – though Paul quickly dismisses this option. The God he proclaims cannot simply be slotted in to the existing patterns of belief.

Paul's speech is often taken as an example of his accommodation to culture, and Paul certainly engages his listeners in terms they understand. His opening greeting 'Men of Athens!' (sometimes translated 'People of Athens' or 'Athenians' – though only men are present) is the formally correct way to address the council, and Paul's speech, even as edited by Luke, contains numerous rhetorical devices that would have impressed his listeners. And Paul cites writings from two Greek philosophers – the *Cretica* of Epimenides from Crete (which he also quotes in Titus 1:12), and the *Phenomena* of Aratus, who came from Paul's home region of Cilicia. This confirms what we might suppose from Paul's own writings, that he was well educated in Greek philosophy and rhetoric as well as being steeped in the Hebrew scriptures.

But we also need to note the manner of Paul's engagement. He begins by highlighting an inconsistency or incoherence in his listeners' perception of the world – that among all the known and named gods, the true God remains unknown to them. This God, who is magisterial in his power, is also (paradoxically) closer than they realise; Paul is hinting here at the incarnation of Jesus as God's presence on earth. Their whole system of statues and temples is an ignorant falsehood, which calls for repentance – and the lynchpin of Paul's argument is the proof of the resurrection. God's vindication of Jesus overturns human judgements, establishes Jesus as Lord and anticipates the end of the world – and in doing so, confirms the Jewish view of God, the world and humanity, over against the Greek view. Though expressed in cultural clothing, Paul's message is uncompromising in its conceptual challenge.

# 4 The resurrection as a source of theological division

**Acts 22:30—23:11**

Luke is here carefully recording Paul's time in Jerusalem prior to the journey to Rome and the end of his story. Paul has already caused a stir in the city among the Jews, and was about to be flogged by the Roman garrison commander when Paul reveals that he is a Roman citizen. The commander wants to learn more about why Paul is controversial, and so takes him to the Jewish ruling council, the Sanhedrin. The deep divisions and animosity between groups in first-century Judaism recorded by Luke match what we know from other sources, and it is now customary to refer to 'first-century Judaisms' to reflect this diversity.

The main division here is between the Sadducees – the aristocratic rulers who regulated temple worship, oversaw civil government and regulated relations with the Romans (as successors to the Hasmoneans) – and the Pharisees, who were mostly a lay movement concerned with practical questions of holiness. Although, in the gospels, Jesus' main disputes appeared to be with the Pharisees, Jesus' biggest theological differences were actually with the Sadducees. At one point, Jesus even tells both the crowd and his disciples to follow the teaching of the Pharisees (in Matthew 23:3) while he questions the core belief of the Sadducees that there is no resurrection of the dead (Matthew 22:23).

The differences in belief arise from different views of scripture. The Sadducees believed that only the Torah (the first five books of the Old Testament) was scripture, and the idea of resurrection is barely evident there. It is a central notion in the prophetic vision of Ezekiel 37, but only becomes a personal hope in Daniel 12, texts also considered scripture by the Pharisees. Despite the difference of view, for Paul the resurrection is the key theological hope of scripture – and is the heart of his message. Belief in Jesus' bodily resurrection should never be dismissed as a 'juggling trick with bones' as some have done. It is the basis of our hope for the future; it says something fundamental about the importance of the body for human existence; and (as Paul expounds in Romans 6:1–5) it is a central metaphor for the new life of the baptised follower of Jesus. It is not something about which we can 'agree to disagree'.

# 5 The resurrection as the hope of judgement

Acts 24:10–26

Luke continues with his detailed account of Paul's various trials, demonstrating both the opposition he faced, and his steadfast defence before various authorities. We are now in the coastal settlement of Caesarea, residence of the governor of Judea. Felix was governor from AD52, and other sources confirm he was violent, unsympathetic to the Jews and unpredictable – leading to his being recalled by the emperor in AD58.

The trial follows the usual Roman pattern of face-to-face accusation before the judge, after which the defendant offers his *apologia*. Both Tertullus, the accusing lawyer, and Paul in his defence, refer to the followers of Jesus ('Nazarenes', 26:5; 'followers of the way', v. 14) as a 'sect'. The word *hairesis* can have a neutral sense of 'party' or 'group' (as in Acts 5:17), but it more usually has a negative connotation, closer to our derived word 'heresy' (Galatians 5:20; 2 Peter 2:1). Paul refutes the specific accusations of being ritually impure within the temple precincts and the suggestion of causing a riot (of particular interest to the Roman governor). But he then, once again, turns to the theme of continuity that we saw in his earlier speeches, as well as those of Peter and Stephen: he worships 'the God of our ancestors' (v. 14); he believes everything in 'the Law and... the prophets' (v. 14); and he shares their hope of resurrection (v. 15). The claim of ancient belief would be important to Romans, who greeted novelty with suspicion. But he is also arguing against his fellow Jews, claiming that the resurrection of Jesus accords with the Jewish scriptures.

It is particularly interesting that he talks of the 'resurrection of the righteous and the wicked' (v. 15). The image of resurrection in Ezekiel 37 is just of God's people, illustrating God bringing them back to life. The earliest mention of a *universal* resurrection comes in Daniel 12:2, and the purpose is that people might be judged before God. This theological conviction has a very practical outworking: since Paul knows that God is his judge, and that in the resurrection there is vindication for all those who trust in him, he can face accusers of every sort confidently and with a clear conscience. This hope provides Paul with an anchor in the storm of theological debate, personal corruption ('hoping that Paul would offer him a bribe', v. 26) and political turmoil.

# 6 The resurrection as cosmic fulfilment of history

Acts 26:1–23

Two years have passed; the more noble Festus has succeeded Felix as governor (24:27). Festus, unsure what to do and needing advice, has invited Herod Agrippa II, client king over territory to the east of Judea, to help him. Agrippa was the great-grandson of Herod the Great, and the last of the Herodian dynasty to bear the title 'king'. He spent large sums beautifying Jerusalem to curry favour with the Jewish leaders, and had power to appoint the high priests – but his capricious decisions in appointment made him unpopular. In focusing on Paul's appearance before Festus and Agrippa, Luke is doing what he has done from the beginning: describing the Jesus movement not as a local, Jewish issue alone, but locating it on the stage of world history (see Luke 1:5; 2:1; 3:1). Paul's testimony is of truly global significance.

Paul is flattering Agrippa by treating him as a respectable Jew, despite both his ancestry and his unpopularity; he talks inclusively of 'our ancestors' (v. 6) and makes the assumption of faith explicit at the end of his appeal (26:27). As he does so, he expounds the resurrection in three ways. First, he sees it as a test of genuine faith in God: why would anyone who believes in the God of the living, not of the dead (see Luke 20:38) think it impossible for God to have raised Jesus (v. 8)? Second, the resurrection is indeed the fulfilment of 'the promise' of God which was the hope of the people of God from the beginning (the 'twelve tribes', v. 7). In a close parallel to Jesus' explanation on the Emmaus Road (Luke 24:26–27), Paul reiterates that Moses and the prophets anticipate that the Messiah would 'suffer and rise from the dead' (vv. 22–23).

But, in Paul's account of his meeting with Jesus on the Damascus road, he goes even further, to a third perspective. The risen Jesus is not simply a completion of what went before, but a cosmic answer to the questions of all humanity – the light in their darkness, release from the power of Satan, and forgiveness of sins (v. 18). In an important sense, this is the end of history, in that God has – in Jesus and his resurrection – spoken a final word not just to Israel, but to all humanity.

# Guidelines

When reading the gospels and Paul's letters, it is not always evident how central the resurrection of Jesus was to the early proclamation of the first Christian communities. But our survey of Acts shows how consistently important it was in the public communication and defence of the message. The later chapters of Acts are generally less well known than the early and middle sections, but here Luke appears to give us a reliable record of Paul's apologetic defence of himself and his gospel – and the resurrection continues to feature as of central importance.

Even when in quite a different cultural context, one in which the idea of bodily resurrection made little sense, Paul persists in focusing on 'Jesus and the resurrection' as his core message. When given a chance to expand on this, he adapts his style and establishes points of cultural contact – but he does this in order to present as credible a still-challenging message, whose acceptance would have required some significant philosophical rethinking on the part of his listeners. The same is true when Paul is faced with intra-Jewish theological controversy; his commitment to a belief in resurrection remains firm, even when that feeds into existing disputes and differences. Paul is convinced that the risen Jesus is indeed the fulfilment of the promise of God, given to his people in the scriptures of the Old Testament, and that this promise has now spilled out – as prophesied – to be a blessing to those of all nations.

But the resurrection is not merely the content of Paul's message; it also provides the animating motivation for his mission. If Jesus has indeed been raised, then everything has changed. The role of the temple has been transformed, since forgiveness is now through trust in Jesus. The nature of hope has changed, since the resurrection brings the future into the present. Even the status of God's people has moved on, since the message is for all nations and God's people are to be the carriers of that good news. And the resurrection gives Paul his confidence, since he has met the risen Jesus who will be his judge, and who has commissioned him for this task and promised to be with him in it.

**FURTHER READING**

Loveday Alexander, *Acts of the Apostles (People's Bible Commentary)* (BRF, 2006).

Howard Marshall, *Acts (Tyndale New Testament Commentary)* (IVP, 1983).

Mikeal Parsons, *Acts (Paideia Commentary on the New Testament)* (Baker, 2008).

John Proctor, *Acts of God: The message and meaning of the book of Acts* (Grove booklet B49).

Ben Witherington, *The Acts of the Apostles: A socio-rhetorical commentary* (Eerdmans, 1998).

*Overleaf… Guidelines* forthcoming issue | Author profile |
Recommended reading | Order and subscription forms

# *Guidelines* forthcoming issue

DAVID SPRIGGS

Trees are a vital part of our landscape and environment – at least for nearly all of us. They enhance our daily experience aesthetically, some because they change with the seasons – I love the brilliant green leaves of spring and the vibrant colours of autumn but find the skeletal structure of deciduous trees through the winter disturbing – others because they remain unchanged through the seasons. We now know they are a vital part to our ecosystem because they reduce the impact of carbon dioxide and protect species in our rainforests. We take trees for granted at our peril. Neil le Tissier has been fascinated with trees in the Old Testament and he shares his reflections with us in this issue, offering us an unusual set of notes for his first contribution as a *Guidelines* writer.

This issue also covers the time of Pentecost. We have two contributions that are particularly helpful for this Christian festival. The first is from George Wieland, who approaches the Acts of the Apostles (the key text for the day of Pentecost) through a mission/spirituality lens. George brings his own perspective from New Zealand, where he is the Director of Mission Research and Training at Carey Theological College in Auckland. His focus recently has been on developing an intentionally missional approach to the reading of the Bible and on understanding the effect of biblical texts as they are read in different social and cultural locations. He also researches and writes on migration and the church, and the experience of immigrant Christians in New Zealand. However, he has recently returned from an extensive period in Turkey, Greece and Italy to visit sites of significance for the mission narratives of Acts and the letters of the New Testament, to gain a deeper understanding of the contexts of mission in these regions both then and now. We are therefore guaranteed a challenging and insightful time as we see how the early church developed under the direction of the Holy Spirit.

The second is from Kate Bruce, one of whose passions while she has been lecturing at Durham has been to stimulate preachers to be innovative as well as biblically faithful. In her week's notes on the role of the Holy Spirit in communication, we can discover some of the biblical foundations for her approaches.

David Dewey picks up the theme of communication as he helps us think again about how best to read passages from the New Testament in today's context.

Andrew Francis is a new writer for *Guidelines*. He will focus on 'Shalom', bringing to us through the text his insights gleaned from many years involved in mediation processes. A further new writer for *Guidelines* is Conrad Gempf, who lectures at the London School of Theology. He gives us a quick tour of Paul's letter to the Romans.

We have regular contributors also adding their qualities to our readings. Steve Walton continues to take us through the next chapters in Luke's gospel. Carly Crouch uses her biblical scholarship to ensure we can understand Hosea in some depth.

# Author profile: Martin Lee

Several years ago, I suffered a short bout of depression. I was morose, not sleeping, disengaging from people and constantly tired. Fortunately, a doctor friend came alongside and gave me excellent support and treatment. The whole episode made me realise my vulnerability and the coping mechanisms that I needed to put in place. I am so pleased that it is in the past, yet it was also a special period as God spoke more clearly and more often than ever before. Scriptures would pop into my head, providing comfort and challenge at the same time. Two verses in particular meant so much: 'Take my yoke upon you and learn from me, for I am gentle and humble in heart, and you will find rest for your souls' (Matthew 11:29, NIV) and 'He must become greater; I must become less' (John 3:30). They were incredibly familiar verses, yet they had not really impacted me or changed me. As I reflected, meditated and repeated them often, they became part of who I am now. It is so easy to know verses, even learn them, without them ever making the impact that God wants in our lives.

That verses like this popped naturally into my head helped me realise the value of knowing the scriptures through memory verses, personal study, small groups and the excellent Bible teaching that I have received. Jesus exhorted people, 'These are the very scriptures that testify about me' (John 5:39). We need to let God speak and breathe his word into our hearts and minds. God is much more interested in changing us into the likeness of his Son than head knowledge. I'm learning (again) to allow the scriptures to change me and make me more like Christ.

And being Christlike is what it is all about. As someone who has travelled extensively, I have learned so much from my friends in the growing non-western church. I have realised that it is not about being 'western' or even 'middle-class'. We live in an individualistic society and view the scriptures through that lens. Our cultural understanding is governed by the philosopher Descartes: 'I think, therefore I am.' I have been greatly challenged by a Nigerian proverb: 'I am because WE are and, since we are, therefore I am.'

I now realise that the famous passage in Ephesians 6 where Paul tells us to put on the whole armour of God is written in the plural. He is telling us to prepare ourselves like a legion of soldiers to face the challenges of the world, rather than seeing it as an individual command to be prepared, on our own, to face down the forces of evil. When we read this passage in its original context, it challenges the values of our individualistic society and makes us realise the importance of the church. With their focus on community, my non-western friends have helped me to stop and think more about the context of the societies to whom the scriptures were written before applying it to my own. I seek to allow God to challenge my western cultural values so that he can continue to radically change me into his image.

# An extract from
# *Peter's Preaching*

In *Peter's Preaching*, Jeremy Duff reveals how an ancient source describes Mark as Peter's translator to a Greek-speaking world. The book moves on to uncover Peter's thought on the key themes of the Christian message, found distributed throughout the gospel. Jeremy pieces these themes together like a jigsaw to reveal how Peter understood them, and how that understanding helps us to appreciate the radical nature of first-century Christian faith.

'Who told you that?' is an important question. The office gossip and, even worse, the 'Twittersphere', are constantly producing crises, scandals and conspiracies, but most of them melt quickly away as soon as you ask, 'Who told you this?' Of course, this is nothing new: the courts have long since known not to accept evidence that starts, 'A friend of mine met this man in the pub who said…'

So what about Mark's gospel? Who is this Mark? He doesn't introduce himself in the gospel, and he certainly isn't one of the twelve disciples. Was he there when Jesus went around doing all those miracles, or is he the first-century equivalent of a 'friend of a friend who met a man in the pub'?

Fortunately, we have a revealing piece of evidence about the identity of Mark, the man responsible for Mark's gospel. It's a shaft of light from the very earliest days of Christianity, which illuminates the origins of this gospel and, as we shall see, of all the gospels. Furthermore, there is intriguing evidence from the very way in which early Christians wrote – creating a system of abbreviations and adopting the latest technology (which could be described as the ancient world's equivalent of the eBook). When all this evidence is put together with the surprising way that the earliest church used and honoured Mark's gospel, there is a fascinating story to be unearthed.

Our starting point is a revealing snippet of information directly about Mark. It comes from a man called Papias, who was bishop of the city of Hierapolis, Turkey, in the early years of the second century AD. (Hierapolis is close to Colosse and is mentioned in Colossians 4:13. It's the modern-day town of Pamukkale, a popular tourist site because of its hot springs.) Scholars normally date Papias's life to about AD60–130. In comparison, Jesus was most probably crucified in AD30, and Mark's gospel written AD60–65. So Papias was a young man around the time when Mark's gospel began to circulate.

Sadly, Papias's own writings have not been preserved. Much from the ancient world is lost to us, long since having rotted away or been destroyed in one disaster or another. Other than in chance finds, like the Dead Sea Scrolls, authors from that era reach us only if, throughout the many centuries before printing was invented, monks dutifully copied and recopied their work as the originals wore out. That only happened if the writings were highly valued. Unfortunately, Papias seems to have fallen out of favour, condemned by a key authority – the first 'church historian', Eusebius (who finished his work in AD324) – probably because Papias wrote interpretations of the book of Revelation that linked 'the beast' with Rome. This use of symbolic language did not go down well in the Roman imperial church in Eusebius' time.

All is not lost, though, for, in his historical works, the same Eusebius twice quoted Papias's words. First, we can read Papias's description of how he was always seeking out information from Jesus' disciples and those who had personally learnt from them.

*Whenever anyone who had been a follower of the elders came, I would investigate the elders' words – what Andrew or what Peter said, or what Philip or what Thomas or James or what John or Matthew or any other of the Lord's disciples said, and the things which Aristion and John the elder, the disciples of the Lord, were saying.*

Papias' words recorded in Eusebius, *History of the Church*, 39.4

Papias wanted to know! This is hardly surprising: people in the ancient world were just as curious as we are today. Furthermore, this was still about a century before any real concept of the 'New Testament' emerged, so a man like Papias had no ready-made source of accepted, authoritative books to rely on. For comparison, we see a similar focus on seeking out accurate sources for what Jesus did and said in the opening four verses of Luke's gospel: Luke searched out the eyewitnesses to Jesus, so that his readers could be assured that they were hearing the truth.

You'll notice that the word 'elder' occurs three times in this quotation. It's a difficult word to pin down. It really means an 'old respected man' but the word was also used for a Christian leader, and, when you read what Papias says, it is clear that he is using it to talk about Jesus' disciples – Andrew, Peter, James and John and others. Peter uses the same word to describe himself in 1 Peter 5:1–2, where he also exhorts the 'elders' of the churches to shepherd God's flock willingly and eagerly.

So whenever someone who had learnt from one of Jesus' disciples (a 'follower of the elders') came to Hierapolis, Papias would ask them about what the disciples had said. This makes sense, for some of Jesus' disciples would certainly have lived until about AD60 or 70, and there would have been people still around in AD100, who had heard them. By AD100, Papias himself would perhaps have been 30 or 40. Indeed, if he was born in AD60, he himself would have been just contemporary with Jesus' disciples, although he would have been only a child and perhaps none of them ever came to Hierapolis in person. (There was a tradition in the early church that Papias heard the apostle John, who is said to have been the last apostle to die. Maybe he did, but Papias' own words here don't make this claim: he states only that he listened to the people who had learnt from the disciples.)

*To order a copy of this book, please use the order form on page 149.*

# Recommended reading

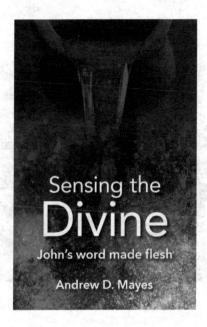

This compelling, inspiring book is an invigorating rereading of the fourth gospel. Uniquely, it approaches John's gospel by exploring how he uses the senses, both physical and spiritual, in his encounter with Jesus Christ, the Word made flesh. This refreshing appreciation of the gospel will activate and stimulate our own discoveries and spiritual quest, not only of the gospel, but also of God's world, ourselves and our mission.

**Sensing the Divine**
*John's word made flesh*
Andrew D. Mayes
978 0 85746 658 7  £10.99  published 19 April 2019
**brfonline.org.uk**

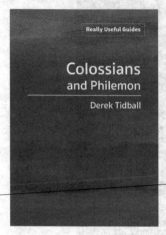
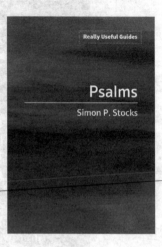

Each Really Useful Guide focuses on a specific biblical book, making it come to life for the contemporary reader, enabling them to understand the message and apply its truth to today's circumstances. Though not a commentary, it gives valuable insight into the book's message. Though not an introduction, it summarises the important aspects of the book to aid reading and application.

**Really Useful Guides: Colossians and Philemon** by Derek Tidball
**Really Useful Guides: Psalms** by Simon Stocks

Colossians and Philemon: 978 0 85746 730 0  £5.99
Psalms: 978 0 85746 731 7  £6.99

**brfonline.org.uk**

# To order

**Online: brfonline.org.uk**
**Telephone: +44 (0)1865 319700**
**Mon–Fri 9.15–17.30**

Delivery times within the UK are normally
15 working days. Prices are correct at the time of
going to press but may change without prior notice.

| Title | Price | Qty | Total |
|---|---|---|---|
| Peter's Preaching | £9.99 | | |
| Sensing the Divine | £10.99 | | |
| Really Useful Guides: Colossians and Philemon | £5.99 | | |
| Really Useful Guides: Psalms | £6.99 | | |
| At Home in Lent | £8.99 | | |
| Celtic Lent | £8.99 | | |

| POSTAGE AND PACKING CHARGES | | | |
|---|---|---|---|
| Order value | UK | Europe | Rest of world |
| Under £7.00 | £2.00 | £5.00 | £7.00 |
| £7.00–£29.99 | £3.00 | £9.00 | £15.00 |
| £30.00 and over | FREE | £9.00 + 15% of order value | £15.00 + 20% of order value |

| | |
|---|---|
| Total value of books | |
| Postage and packing | |
| Total for this order | |

**Please complete in BLOCK CAPITALS**

Title ............ First name/initials ...................... Surname ...............................................

Address.................................................................................................................

..........................................................................................Postcode..........................

Acc. No. ................................................ Telephone ...............................................

Email.....................................................................................................................

## Method of payment

☐ Cheque (made payable to BRF)   ☐ MasterCard / Visa

Card no. ☐☐☐☐ ☐☐☐☐ ☐☐☐☐ ☐☐☐☐ ☐☐☐☐ ☐☐☐☐

Valid from M M Y Y  Expires M M Y Y  Security code* ☐☐☐

Last 3 digits on the reverse of the card

Signature* .................................................................... Date ............/............/............

*ESSENTIAL IN ORDER TO PROCESS YOUR ORDER

**Please return this form to:** BRF, 15 The Chambers, Vineyard, Abingdon OX14 3FE | enquiries@brf.org.uk
To read our terms and find out about cancelling your order, please visit brfonline.org.uk/terms.

The Bible Reading Fellowship (BRF) is a Registered Charity (233280)

# How to encourage Bible reading in your church

BRF has been helping individuals connect with the Bible for over 90 years. We want to support churches as they seek to encourage church members into regular Bible reading.

### Order a Bible reading resources pack

This pack is designed to give your church the tools to publicise our Bible reading notes. It includes:

- Sample Bible reading notes for your congregation to try.
- Publicity resources, including a poster.
- A church magazine feature about Bible reading notes.

The pack is free, but we welcome a £5 donation to cover the cost of postage. If you require a pack to be sent outside the UK or require a specific number of sample Bible reading notes, please contact us for postage costs. More information about what the current pack contains is available on our website.

### How to order and find out more

- Visit **biblereadingnotes.org.uk/for-churches**
- Telephone BRF on +44 (0)1865 319700 Mon–Fri 9.15–17.30
- Write to us at BRF, 15 The Chambers, Vineyard, Abingdon OX14 3FE

### Keep informed about our latest initiatives

We are continuing to develop resources to help churches encourage people into regular Bible reading, wherever they are on their journey. Join our email list at **biblereadingnotes.org.uk/helpingchurches** to stay informed about the latest initiatives that your church could benefit from.

### Introduce a friend to our notes

We can send information about our notes and current prices for you to pass on. Please contact us.

# Transforming lives and communities

BRF is a charity that is passionate about making a difference through the Christian faith. We want to see lives and communities transformed through our creative programmes and resources for individuals, churches and schools. We are doing this by resourcing:

- **Christian growth and understanding of the Bible.** Through our Bible reading notes, books, digital resources, Quiet Days and other events, we're resourcing individuals, groups and leaders in churches for their own spiritual journey and for their ministry.
- **Church outreach in the local community.** BRF is the home of two programmes that churches are embracing to great effect as they seek to engage with their local communities: Messy Church and The Gift of Years.
- **Teaching Christianity in primary schools.** Our Barnabas in Schools team is working with primary-aged children and their teachers, enabling them to explore Christianity creatively and confidently within the school curriculum.
- **Children's and family ministry.** Through our Parenting for Faith programme, websites and published resources, we're working with churches and families, enabling children and adults alike to explore Christianity creatively and bring the Bible alive.

## Do you share our vision?

Sales of our books and Bible reading notes cover the cost of producing them. However, our other programmes are funded primarily by donations, grants and legacies. If you share our vision, would you help us to transform even more lives and communities? Your prayers and financial support are vital for the work that we do. You could:

- support BRF's ministry with a regular donation (at **brf.org.uk/donate**);
- support us with a one-off gift (use the form on pages 153–54);
- consider leaving a gift to BRF in your will (see page 152);
- encourage your church to support BRF as part of your church's giving to home mission – perhaps focusing on a specific area of our ministry, or a particular member of our Barnabas in Schools team.
- most important of all, support BRF with your prayers.

# Giving for the future

The feast day of St Finan is celebrated on 17 February. Now largely lost within the Anglican tradition, feast days are an annual celebration of a saint, usually marked by prayers and a relevant Bible reading.

Finan lived during the seventh century AD and became bishop of Lindisfarne when Aidan, the founder of the now-famous monastery, died. In his book, *40 Days with the Celtic Saints: Devotional readings for a time of preparation* (BRF, 2017), David Cole writes:

> Finan's heart for mission, as well as his tenacity in his belief, marked him out as a great man of faith and inner strength. His influence spread throughout England...

In 2004, a church near Portsmouth with a 'heart for mission' stepped out into the unknown and launched the first Messy Church. They had no idea that 15 years later its influence would spread not only throughout England but also around the world. Today, there are almost 4,000 Messy Churches in over 25 countries.

BRF is the home of Messy Church, and through it we are helping families become followers of Jesus. For almost a century, we have been able to fund the growth, development and sustainability of programmes like Messy Church, thanks to the generosity of those who support us through gifts in wills.

If you share our vision for transforming lives through the Christian faith, would you consider leaving a gift in your will to BRF? It doesn't need to be huge to help us make a real difference.

For further information about making a gift to BRF in your will, please visit **brf.org.uk/lastingdifference**, contact Sophie Aldred on **+44 (0)1865 319700** or email **giving@brf.org.uk**.

**Whatever you can do or give, we thank you for your support.**

## SHARING OUR VISION – MAKING A GIFT

**I would like to make a gift to support BRF. Please use my gift for:**

☐ where it is needed most ☐ Barnabas in Schools ☐ Parenting for Faith
☐ Messy Church ☐ The Gift of Years

| Title | First name/initials | Surname |
|-------|---------------------|---------|
| | | |

| Address | |
|---------|---|
| | Postcode |

| Email |
|-------|

| Telephone |
|-----------|

| Signature | Date |
|-----------|------|

*giftaid it* You can add an extra 25p to every £1 you give.

**Please treat as Gift Aid donations all qualifying gifts of money made**

☐ today, ☐ in the past four years, ☐ and in the future.

I am a UK taxpayer and understand that if I pay less Income Tax and/or Capital Gains Tax in the current tax year than the amount of Gift Aid claimed on all my donations, it is my responsibility to pay any difference.

☐ My donation does not qualify for Gift Aid.

Please notify BRF if you want to cancel this Gift Aid declaration, change your name or home address, or no longer pay sufficient tax on your income and/or capital gains.

Please complete other side of form ➡

**Please return this form to:**
BRF, 15 The Chambers, Vineyard, Abingdon OX14 3FE

The Bible Reading Fellowship is a Registered Charity (233280)

## SHARING OUR VISION – MAKING A GIFT

### Regular giving

**By Direct Debit:** You can set up a Direct Debit quickly and easily at **brf.org.uk/donate**

**By Standing Order:** Please contact our Fundraising Administrator +44 (0)1235 462305 | giving@brf.org.uk

### One-off donation

Please accept my gift of:

☐ £10 ☐ £50 ☐ £100 Other £ ⬚

by (delete as appropriate):

☐ Cheque/Charity Voucher payable to 'BRF'

☐ MasterCard/Visa/Debit card/Charity card

Name on card

Card no. ⬚⬚⬚⬚ ⬚⬚⬚⬚ ⬚⬚⬚⬚ ⬚⬚⬚⬚

Valid from ⬚⬚/⬚⬚ Expires ⬚⬚/⬚⬚

Security code* ⬚⬚⬚ *Last 3 digits on the reverse of the card
ESSENTIAL IN ORDER TO PROCESS YOUR PAYMENT

Signature                                    Date

☐ I would like to leave a gift in my will to BRF.

For more information, visit **brf.org.uk/lastingdifference**

For help or advice regarding making a gift, please contact our Fundraising Administrator +44 (0)1235 462305

↩ Please complete other side of form

**Please return this form to:**
BRF, 15 The Chambers, Vineyard, Abingdon OX14 3FE

**BRF**

GL0119

# GUIDELINES SUBSCRIPTION RATES

Please note our new subscription rates, current until 30 April 2020:

### Individual subscriptions
covering 3 issues for under 5 copies, payable in advance
(including postage & packing):

|  | UK | Europe | Rest of world |
| --- | --- | --- | --- |
| *Guidelines* 1-year subscription | £17.40 | £25.50 | £29.40 |
| *Guidelines* 3-year subscription (9 issues) | £49.50 | N/A | N/A |

### Group subscriptions
covering 3 issues for 5 copies or more, sent to **one** UK address (post free):

*Guidelines* 1-year subscription          £13.80 per set of 3 issues p.a.

Please note that the annual billing period for group subscriptions runs from 1 May to 30 April.

### Overseas group subscription rates
Available on request. Please email **enquiries@brf.org.uk**.

Copies may also be obtained from Christian bookshops:

*Guidelines*                              £4.60 per copy

---

All our Bible reading notes can be ordered online by visiting
**biblereadingnotes.org.uk/subscriptions**

For information about our other Bible reading notes,
and apps for iPhone and iPod touch, visit
**biblereadingnotes.org.uk**

## GUIDELINES INDIVIDUAL SUBSCRIPTION FORM

All our Bible reading notes can be ordered online by visiting
**biblereadingnotes.org.uk/subscriptions**

☐ I would like to take out a subscription:

Title ............... First name/initials ............... Surname ...............................................

Address ...................................................................................................................

............................................................................ Postcode ...............................

Telephone ............................... Email .......................................................................

Please send *Guidelines* beginning with the May 2019 / September 2019 / January 2020 issue (*delete as appropriate*):

| (*please tick box*) | UK | Europe | Rest of world |
|---|---|---|---|
| *Guidelines* 1-year subscription | ☐ £17.40 | ☐ £25.50 | ☐ £29.40 |
| *Guidelines* 3-year subscription | ☐ £49.50 | N/A | N/A |

Total enclosed £ ......................... (cheques should be made payable to 'BRF')

Please charge my MasterCard / Visa ☐ Debit card ☐ with £ .......................

Card no. ☐☐☐☐ ☐☐☐☐ ☐☐☐☐ ☐☐☐☐

Valid from ☐☐/☐☐    Expires ☐☐/☐☐    Security code* ☐☐☐

Last 3 digits on the reverse of the card

Signature* ........................................................................ Date ....../....../......

*ESSENTIAL IN ORDER TO PROCESS YOUR PAYMENT

**To set up a Direct Debit**, please also complete the Direct Debit instruction on page 159 and return it to BRF with this form.

**Please return this form with the appropriate payment to:**
BRF, 15 The Chambers, Vineyard, Abingdon OX14 3FE

To read our terms and find out about cancelling your order, please visit **brfonline.org.uk/terms**.

The Bible Reading Fellowship (BRF) is a Registered Charity (233280)

GL0119

## GUIDELINES GIFT SUBSCRIPTION FORM

☐ I would like to give a gift subscription (please provide both names and addresses):

Title _____ First name/initials _____ Surname _____

Address _____

_____ Postcode _____

Telephone _____ Email _____

Gift subscription name _____

Gift subscription address _____

_____ Postcode _____

Gift message (20 words max. or include your own gift card):

_____

_____

Please send *Guidelines* beginning with the May 2019 / September 2019 / January 2020 issue (*delete as appropriate*):

| (*please tick box*) | UK | Europe | Rest of world |
|---|---|---|---|
| *Guidelines* 1-year subscription | ☐ £17.40 | ☐ £25.50 | ☐ £29.40 |
| *Guidelines* 3-year subscription | ☐ £49.50 | N/A | N/A |

Total enclosed £ _____ (cheques should be made payable to 'BRF')

Please charge my MasterCard / Visa ☐ Debit card ☐ with £ _____

Card no. ☐☐☐☐ ☐☐☐☐ ☐☐☐☐ ☐☐☐☐

Valid from ☐☐☐☐ Expires ☐☐☐☐ Security code* ☐☐☐

Last 3 digits on the reverse of the card

Signature* _____ Date _____/_____/_____

*ESSENTIAL IN ORDER TO PROCESS YOUR PAYMENT

**To set up a Direct Debit**, please also complete the Direct Debit instruction on page 159 and return it to BRF with this form.

**Please return this form with the appropriate payment to:**
BRF, 15 The Chambers, Vineyard, Abingdon OX14 3FE

To read our terms and find out about cancelling your order, please visit **brfonline.org.uk/terms**.

The Bible Reading Fellowship (BRF) is a Registered Charity (233280)

## DIRECT DEBIT PAYMENT

You can pay for your annual subscription to our Bible reading notes using Direct Debit. You need only give your bank details once, and the payment is made automatically every year until you cancel it. If you would like to pay by Direct Debit, please use the form opposite, entering your BRF account number under 'Reference number'.

You are fully covered by the Direct Debit Guarantee:

### The Direct Debit Guarantee

- This Guarantee is offered by all banks and building societies that accept instructions to pay Direct Debits.

- If there are any changes to the amount, date or frequency of your Direct Debit, The Bible Reading Fellowship will notify you 10 working days in advance of your account being debited or as otherwise agreed. If you request The Bible Reading Fellowship to collect a payment, confirmation of the amount and date will be given to you at the time of the request.

- If an error is made in the payment of your Direct Debit, by The Bible Reading Fellowship or your bank or building society, you are entitled to a full and immediate refund of the amount paid from your bank or building society.

- If you receive a refund you are not entitled to, you must pay it back when The Bible Reading Fellowship asks you to.

- You can cancel a Direct Debit at any time by simply contacting your bank or building society. Written confirmation may be required. Please also notify us.

The Bible Reading Fellowship

# Instruction to your bank or building society to pay by Direct Debit

Please fill in the whole form using a ballpoint pen and return it to:
BRF, 15 The Chambers, Vineyard, Abingdon OX14 3FE

Service User Number:

| 5 | 5 | 8 | 2 | 2 | 9 |
|---|---|---|---|---|---|

Name and full postal address of your bank or building society

| To: The Manager | Bank/Building Society |
|---|---|
| Address | |
| | |
| | |
| | Postcode |

Name(s) of account holder(s)

Branch sort code

Bank/Building Society account number

Reference number

## Instruction to your Bank/Building Society
Please pay The Bible Reading Fellowship Direct Debits from the account detailed
in this instruction, subject to the safeguards assured by the Direct Debit Guarantee.
I understand that this instruction may remain with The Bible Reading Fellowship and, if so,
details will be passed electronically to my bank/building society.

Signature(s)

Banks and Building Societies may not accept Direct Debit instructions for some types
of account.

# BRF

# Transforming
## lives and communities

## Christian growth and understanding of the Bible

Resourcing individuals, groups and leaders in churches for their own
spiritual journey and for their ministry

## Church outreach in the local community

Offering two programmes that churches
are embracing to great effect as they
seek to engage with their local
communities and transform lives

## Teaching Christianity in primary schools

Working with children and teachers to explore Christianity creatively
and confidently

## Children's and family ministry

Working with churches and families to explore
Christianity creatively and bring the Bible alive   **parenting for faith**

Visit **brf.org.uk** for more information on BRF's work

brf.org.uk